Autodidactic:

Self-Taught

BY

James W. Parkinson

Genesis Press, Inc.

Genesis Press, Inc.
200 6th St N Suite 601
Columbus MS 39701

Autodidactic: Self-Taught Copyright © 2009 James W. Parkinson

ISBN 13: 978-1-58571-425-4
ISBN 10:1-58571-425-9

First Printing September 2009
Second Printing February 2010
Third Printing June 2010
Fourth Printing September 2014
Fifth Printing August 2016
Printed in the United States of America

DEDICATION

This book is dedicated to Susan Parkinson—
my wife, best friend, and severest critic.

ACKNOWLEDGEMENTS

I would like to thank all those who helped me with this book. I apologize to those I am sure I have unavoidably and unintentionally overlooked.

I would like to thank my family and friends who helped by reading the manuscripts and making innumerable improvements: my wife, Sue; my children, Krista, Brett, Brooke, and Matthew James; my brother and his wife, Dr. Richard W. Parkinson and Mavis Parkinson; my nephew, Clifford Parkinson; Hassan Jallow, The Honorable Douglas P. Miller, The Honorable Dee Benson, The Honorable V. Manuel Perez, Greg Cervantes, Lee Benson, Steve Hill, Dusty Heuston, Dr. Michael Benson, Kim Clark, Neil F. Dimick, Elaine Hatch, Tim Parrott, Dr. Steven Lake, Joe Ceja, Manuel Arredondo, Rudy Ramirez, Kenneth Young, Gilbert Queen, Omer and Irma Mohamed, Woody Germany, Steve Root, Luis Flores, Laurie Parkinson, Dan Hicks, Ty and Mindy McRae, Danielle Callaway, Walter Fleishhaker, Randi Greene, and my brother Dr. Brett T. Parkinson and his daughter Amelia Parkinson.

I am grateful to those who have served as mentors to me: Sue Parkinson, Tom Anderson, Senator Orrin Hatch, E. Grant Fitts, The Honorable Monroe McKay, Phil Ferantti, and Rod Basehore.

I owe a special debt of gratitude to those I work with on a daily basis: Brooke Parkinson, Ann Hermanson, Mike Montgomery, and Bonnie Kane. Without them this book would never have been written.

Finally, I would like to thank those at Genesis Press: Wilbur Colom, Deborah Schumaker, and Brian Jones.

They are the best in the business.

TABLE OF CONTENTS

FOREWORD

BY
V. MANUEL PEREZ

I cannot tell you the number of people I have met while in public office who have been very successful in the pursuit of wealth but, late in the day, realized that they hadn't really succeeded. On the other hand, I have known people from all walks of life who have dedicated their personal lives to a cause greater than themselves and their own self-interests and have gone on to live a very satisfying life. A great example of this is my dear friend, Jim Parkinson.

In James W. Parkinson's book *Autodidactic: Self-Taught* you will find practical wisdom drawn from his unique personal experiences as an attorney and historical statements issued by some of our world's most remarkable leaders. These are renowned government and community leaders who have shaped our domestic and international policy.

Eileen de los Reyes, one of my professors at the Harvard Graduate School of Education, once said in class that "Literacy is power, if we choose to recognize its world potential." What a wonderful thought!

I must admit, I did not always see it this way. Being the son of immigrant farm workers and growing up in the barrios of Coachella, California—Spanish being my primary language—I only knew what I saw around me. There were bad things, yes, and injustices, but I also had my parent's love, the guidance of close friends and the mentoring of outstanding teachers who all deeply instilled into me the fact that education was the great equalizer. Once I got into high school and especially on into college, I came to eventually realize that, if I followed their advice, I might view the world quite differently. And this new view could be transformative.

I recognized that this would only be the case if I disciplined myself and took the time to embrace the need to learn how to read, write and speak the English language fluently. I came to terms with the fact that, being a citizen of the United States and understanding my parents' struggle to find their place in the American Dream, it was now my responsibility and obligation to become one with my American culture and integrate it into my Mexican culture. In short, I had to learn to appreciate the English language just as much as I appreciated my primary language, Spanish.

Coming full circle, after a few years of sunrises and full moons, I now find myself serving as an Assemblyman in the 80th Assembly District where, every day, I remind myself why I am here and what my purpose is in life. I strive to work daily toward a just social and economic society in which all individuals, no matter their race, ethnic, religious or sexual background, have equal opportunity and have sufficient support to be assertive and voice their minds when necessary. I have come to the conclusion that my Harvard Professor de los Reyes and Jim Parkinson are correct; "Literacy is power, if we so choose to recognize its potential."

Jim Parkinson hits the mark when he states, "Events that are written give birth to thoughts that change behavior and shape our soul." *Autodidactic* is a powerful book. I believe it will make a real difference in our communities. I am both privileged and honored to have James Parkinson as my mentor and personal friend.

Victor Manuel Perez

The Honorable Victor Manuel Perez formerly represented the 80th Assembly District in the California State Legislature. He is the proud product of the Coachella Valley Unified School District system, completed his Bachelor of Arts Degree at the University of California, Riverside, and earned his Master's Degree in Education from Harvard University, Cambridge, Massachusetts.

PROLOGUE

We have it in our power to begin the world over again.–
Thomas Paine

"Jimmy, do you want to be as ignorant today as you were yesterday?"

Every morning, between the time I get up and the time I leave my house, I look into the bathroom mirror and ask myself that question.

"Ignorant: (ig´- nər - ənt) adj. 1. Without education or knowledge. 2. Exhibiting lack of education or knowledge: *an ignorant mistake.* 3. Unaware or uninformed: *ignorant of what had happened….* " (*The American Heritage Dictionary, Second College Edition*)

I may not be able to control many things, but I have learned I am able to control my level of ignorance.

I've titled the book *Autodidactic: Self-Taught*, but please don't think my using such an obscure word means I think I have reached the pinnacle of success and now want to "preach" to the "self-help" book buyers who haunt the Barnes & Noble and Borders stores of America looking for the book that will give them a quick fix. There are no shortcuts to achieving one's potential. This is a lifelong challenge that needs to be thought about carefully and executed with discipline and steadfastness.

I was not a child prodigy. As a matter of fact, my first memory of a teaching moment, albeit informal, was not in a classroom but in the tiny living room of my parents' apartment at 73 E. Stadium Place, in New Orleans, LA. They lived in married student housing at Tulane University. I was four years old. My mother handed me a copy of *Life* magazine and told me to circle every word I recognized. I still remember the only two words I circled: "the" and "I."

During the next fifteen years I attended school, played basketball, made friends, and eventually graduated, with fairly good grades, from high school. Some classes I liked, others I didn't, but by and large I enjoyed going to school in the small town in southern California where we then lived. I read only what I was forced to read—and sometimes I didn't even do that. I remember we were assigned John Steinbeck's classic, *The Grapes of Wrath*, in English IV my senior year, but I never finished it. Another book assigned but never read was *The Heart of Darkness*, by Joseph Conrad. If the movie versions of these classics hadn't been shown in class, I would have never passed English IV.

Why didn't I read them when I should have? More importantly, why didn't I understand the importance of language study in general and reading in particular? Where were my grammar school and high school teachers? Why couldn't they inspire me? Where was I? After giving these questions a lifetime of thought, I am convinced that my inability to engage intellectually in elementary, junior high and high school can be traced to several painful childhood experiences, uninspired teachers, my own intellectual laziness, and to one word—"embarrassment."

I have a couple of rather vivid and painful memories of my childhood that have informed, to a certain extent, my early reluctance to engage intellectually. I am a Mormon, and at the age of seven I attended a Sunday School class for kids my own age in a Women's Club building that was used as a chapel in Coachella, California. At that time my family was living a few miles down the road in Indio. We had just moved to town. I didn't know anybody. The teacher had the class sit in a circle. It was my first Sunday in this brand-new environment and, out of nowhere, the teacher handed me a Bible and asked me to read a verse. I panicked. I became extraordinarily self-conscious and made mistake after painful mistake as I tried to read. Finally the teacher took the Bible out of my hands and gave it to another boy to finish the verse I had been massacring. I was totally humiliated— yet I had to go back to that class again and again.

Spelling was another early mystery to me. I never learned the rules or, for that matter, the fact that there were rules. My inability to spell explains in part my poor penmanship. My thinking went something like this: If a teacher couldn't read my writing, how could she tell I didn't know how to spell? But by the third grade everybody could tell I was struggling. How do I remember that some fifty years later? Because the one time I got a perfect score on a weekly spelling test, my teacher announced it in front of the whole class and they all clapped. I put my head on the desk and cried.

In the sixth grade at Jackson Elementary School the teacher did his best to teach a group of us the fundamentals of the English language. For some reason, I have a clear memory of a sheet of paper being passed out to every student that listed verbs and their tenses. I ran yesterday, I run today, tomorrow

I will run. The list was exhaustive. It overwhelmed me. I just knew I could not learn all the different ways to use words. I was so intimidated by it that I didn't even take the list home to study.

As I look back on my educational experiences, I am sure I had many dedicated and fine teachers. Unfortunately, however, none of them ever inspired me to become a true learner. If I am truthful with myself, I know that I am critical of my teachers. But the person I am the most disappointed in is myself.

One more story and we will leave my childhood behind. My mother sang and played the piano. She thought it would be wonderful if I could learn to play a musical instrument. I picked the guitar and she picked the teacher. When I arrived at the teacher's house it was immediately clear, even to an eight-year-old, that he was anything but a professional music teacher. For one thing, there was really no place in his house for a lesson. Even though I was too young really to expect anything, e.g., a studio or a soundproof room, in retrospect sitting on opposite twin beds in the back bedroom of a tract house should have been a sufficient clue this music experience was going nowhere. Which is exactly where it went!

In the first five minutes I was there, the teacher had me holding the guitar and strumming "chords." He gave no explanation as to what I was doing or why I was doing it. "Just play the chords, Jimmy," he said. I was confused. After the lesson I was sent home with a sheet of music and told to practice one half hour a day. I did this religiously for an entire week. I would look at the paper, move the fingers of my left hand and work the pick with my right hand. I had no idea what I was doing or why. I quit my music lessons after a month of pure, unadulterated frustration.

This is neither a religious nor spiritual book, but before we go much further I would like to share a couple of thoughts that have informed, and continue to inform, my worldview. I have been a trial lawyer for over thirty-two years and have taken, literally, thousands of depositions under oath. I forget most witnesses and their testimonies as soon as the case is over. But a man I met over twenty years ago was so remarkable, and his accomplishments so singular, that my time with him is indelibly impressed on my memory. It was not what Captain Eugene Cernan, one of our earliest astronauts, said during his deposition that has stayed with me all these years, it is what he said during the hour afterwards that made a lasting impression.

I first met Captain Cernan in 1989, in a conference room at a hotel located just outside the city limits of San Francisco, California. He had been on the board of directors of Technical Equities, and my clients were suing the company, its bankers, accountants and lawyers. I had become friendly over the course of the litigation with Captain Cernan's attorney, so after the deposition I felt comfortable enough to ask if I could talk to his client about his experience as an astronaut. I wanted to find out what it was like to walk on the moon. Had I known how his words would impress me, I would have asked the court reporter to have taken down our conversation. Fortunately, Captain Eugene Cernan wrote a book in 1999 entitled *The Last Man On The Moon*, where he again shared the thoughts that had so impressed me:

> ...looking back at Earth, I saw only a distant blue-and-white star. There were oceans down there, deep and wide, but I could see completely across them now and they seemed so small. However deep, however wide, the sea has a shore and a bottom. Out where I was dashing through space, I was wrapped in infin-

ity. Even the word 'infinity' lost meaning, because I couldn't measure it, and without sunsets and sunrises, time meant nothing more than performing some checklist function at a specific point in the mission. Beyond that star over there, Alpheratz, is another and another. And over there, beyond Nunki, the same thing. Behind Formalhaut, even more stars, stretching beyond my imagination. Stars and eternal distant blackness everywhere. *There is no end.* I'm not an overly religious person, but I certainly am a believer, and when I looked around, I saw beauty, not emptiness. No one in their right mind can see such a sight and deny the spirituality of the experience, nor the existence of a Supreme Being, whether their God be Buddha or Jesus Christ or Whoever. The name is less important than the acceptance of a Creator. Someone, some being, some power placed our little world, our Sun and our Moon where they are in the dark void, and the scheme defies any attempt at logic. It is just too perfect and beautiful to have happened by accident. I can't tell you how or why it exists in this special way, only that it does, and I know that for certain because I have been out there and I have seen the endlessness of space and time with my own eyes.

It was not by accident that we three veteran spacemen had John Magee's 'High Flight' poem aboard *Apollo 10*, for there were indeed moments when I honestly felt that I could reach out my hand, just as he said, and touch the face of God.[1]

Captain Cernan was exactly what you'd imagine an astronaut to be: He sat ramrod straight and answered questions with authority and without fear or hesitation. What struck me, however, was the reflective, philosophical and contemplative side to his nature. Reading Captain Cernan's description of the earth as seen from the moon, I am more convinced than ever that I am not an accident…and neither are you.

When I returned home after speaking with him—this last man to walk on the moon—I could not wait to share the experience with my father. As I told my dad about my hour with the astronaut, he in turn told me how in 1927 his own father had taken him to see Charles Lindbergh, the first man to fly an airplane, *The Spirit of St. Louis*, solo across the Atlantic. As I went to bed that night I couldn't help but reflect on how lucky my dad and I both had been and how little time (sixty-two years) separated our experiences. It is staggering to think how much can be accomplished in so short a period of time.

I was raised in a religious home, so questions as to why we are here on earth have always been a topic for discussion in my family. I don't want this to be a religious tract designed either overtly or covertly to convert anyone to any religion. But Captain Cernan's experience does cause even the least religious person to pause and wonder about the purpose of life.

No one who really knows me would call me an orthodox Mormon. I hate sitting through three hours of meetings on Sundays. I even hate doing it on Christmas and Easter. Although I consider my two-year church mission in Argentina, when I was nineteen years old, to be the watershed moment in my life, I don't want to serve another mission. I have done that. If there is, however, one tenet of Mormon doctrine that is and has been the motivating force behind my intellectual life and the impetus for this book, it is found in *The Doctrine and Covenants*, section 130, verses 18-19:[2]

18. Whatever principle of intelligence we attain unto in this life, it will rise with us in the resurrection.

19. And if a person gains more knowledge and intelligence in this

life through his diligence and obedience than another, he will
have so much the advantage in the world to come.

Although inspired by the aforementioned religious text,
my love of learning has a very practical and pragmatic appli-
cation: I want a well-paying job. I also realize that ignorance
is truly unattractive in a man or woman, and overexposure to
it in a relationship is not only annoying, it can also be downright toxic. I remember when I was a seventeen-year-old
freshman in college I once asked a *drop-dead* good looking
co-ed to join me for a movie in Salt Lake City. The movie was
Gone With the Wind—the Academy Award-winning film set
during the American Civil War. The evening was going great
until the girl snuggled up to me and whispered, "I can't stand
it, who wins the war?" When the lights came on in the the-
ater—and I thought about what she had said—she just wasn't
that attractive anymore. Furthermore, I have never met a
woman who, after ten years of marriage, wants the only oral
communication with her husband to be: "Hey, what time
does the game start?" and "Can you bring me and the boys
another beer?"

Why did I write this book? Because I recently read that
there are over thirty million adults in America who cannot
read. It is a myth that America is a literate country. True literacy requires commitment, and we have become a country
obsessed with instant gratification and a spectator mental-
ity. Why write this book? Because employers complain that
their employees can't write a simple memo or read and follow
simple instructions. Why write this book? Because America
is starting to produce a generation of athletes who get their
competitive advantage from a vial and not from discipline
and focused effort. I believe, we, as adults, owe it to our children to tell them the truth about what they must know to

become successful in life. We owe it to our children to tell them that education is their responsibility, and it will require effort and hard work.

I wrote this book because I want to share with you how I became me and hopefully inspire you to take responsibility for your own life and understand the magic of "being self-taught." I did it the hard way. I made a lot of mistakes and had to make adjustments. I didn't start out *Magna Cum Laude*. I failed first and was remarkably off-track early on. But my journey has been worth it. There is too much at stake for me to keep my experiences a secret. I don't want you to stumble in the darkness and possibly fail. Failure in itself is not a bad thing—but it should be a temporary thing, not a lifetime commitment.

Before we get to an in-depth discussion of vocabulary, reading and writing, I want to remind us all of the importance of discipline and perseverance in our lives. We sometimes blame our failures on a "bad gene pool" or "bad luck." Is this what the Romans taught us?

In his book, *The Decline and Fall of the Roman Empire*, Edward Gibbon described the discipline demanded of the Roman soldiers and the rigorous training they received. But this training made them the most feared and effective military men of their era:

> And yet so sensible were the Romans of the imperfection of valor without skill and practice that, in their language, the name of an army, (i.e., exercitus), was borrowed from the word which signified exercise. Military exercises were the important and unremitted object of their discipline. The recruits and young soldiers were constantly trained, both in the morning and in the evening, nor was age or knowledge allowed to excuse the veterans from the daily repetition of what they had completely learnt...and it was carefully observed that the arms destined to this imitation of war should be of double the weight which was required in real

action…Such were the arts of war by which the Roman emperors defended their extensive conquests, and preserved a military spirit, at a time when every other virtue was oppressed by luxury and despotism.[3]

This basic principle of hard work and its relationship to success was again reaffirmed more than a millennium after the Romans abandoned their core values and "fell." In his 2008 book, *Talent Is Overrated*, Geoff Colvin explains:

> …Great performance is in our hands far more than most of us ever suspected.[4]

> …Surviving manuscripts show that Mozart was constantly revising, reworking, crossing out and rewriting whole sections, jotting down fragments and putting them aside for months or years.[5]

> …neither Tiger [Woods] nor his father suggested that Tiger came into this world with a gift for golf. Earl did not believe that Tiger was an ordinary kid (but, then, parents hardly ever believe that). He thought Tiger had an unusual ability to understand what he was told and to keep track of numbers, even before he could count very high. Tiger has repeatedly credited his father for his success. Trying to understand his early interest in the game, he has not invoked an inborn fascination. Rather, he has written, 'golf for me was an apparent attempt to emulate the person I looked up to more than anyone: my father.' Asked to explain Tiger's phenomenal success, father and son always give the same reason: hard work.[6]

> …no one, not even the most 'talented' performers, became great without at least ten years of very hard preparation.[7]

Although I have had some remarkable teachers in my life, I consider myself an autodidact who, every day, is trying to beat the clock and learn as much as he can. You will read my story in the following pages—at least the part of my story that I think you will find relevant and, hopefully, helpful. In Chapter 4 you will meet Hassan Jallow—one of the most impressive men I have ever met. Mr. Jallow is a former Justice of the Supreme Court of The Gambia and the former Chief

Prosecutor at the International Criminal Tribunal for Rwanda, which today sits in Arusha, Tanzania. My interview with this remarkable man will give you insight into the impact learning to read had on his life and will, hopefully, inspire and influence us all to follow this "modified" admonition of Thomas L. Friedman to "put away the Game Boys, turn off the television set, put away the iPod…" and open a book.[8]

If I am to heed Thomas Paine's admonition and begin my "world over again," I must not only ask myself every morning, "Jimmy, do you want to be as ignorant today as you were yesterday?"—but I must also leave behind the image of the person I am today, and consciously make an effort to better educate myself for all my tomorrows and for eternity. In the pages that follow I will share with you how I have done this for the last forty years by expanding my vocabulary, reading voraciously, and by making writing a part of my daily life. Hopefully, by showing you how I became me, I can help you become a better you and together we can begin, one by one, to make this "world over again."

CHAPTER 1

VOCABULARY

I saw that the best thing I could do was get hold of a dictionary—to study, to learn some words. –Malcolm X

A Sunday school teacher, a third grade teacher, a music teacher, and a well-intentioned sixth grade teacher all made lasting impressions on me. But the overwhelming amount of the material, uninspiring and incompetent instructors, and, more importantly, my lack of motivation slowed my intellectual growth. I didn't want to be made fun of, so I never tried. If you don't try—you don't fail. If you don't fail—nobody laughs at you. That was my reasoning, so I became a very good basketball player and a great talker. Back then, I thought that I didn't need to read or spell; I was clever enough to succeed with limited knowledge. This way of thinking came to an abrupt end when I landed in Buenos Aires, Argentina, in January of 1969.

Before arriving in Argentina for my two-year mission for the Mormon Church, I studied Spanish for three months at the Language Training Center in Provo, Utah. With that background and my two years of high school Spanish, I was not cocky, but I was confident I could manage. But studying a foreign language in a sterile classroom in America and being immersed in it in a foreign country are two entirely different experiences. I learned this right away. Upon landing at Ezeiza Airport in Buenos Aires I was starving, so I approached a food counter and tried to buy something to eat. I found out that I didn't have the words in Spanish for what I wanted so what I ended up eating was something I pointed to. To make matters worse, I wasn't sure what it cost. Not only did I not have a working Spanish *vocabulary*, but also I had zero knowledge of Argentine currency!

Everybody in Argentina spoke so fast—700 words a minute with gusts up to 975, or so I thought. It would be months before I understood enough even to realize that the Porteños of Buenos Aires have an accent that is peculiar to the capital and not used anywhere else in the country. I found out in Córdoba, my next destination, that its citizens also had their own distinct lilt that is charming if you are familiar with it and downright unintelligible and annoying if you weren't.

Shortly after arriving in Argentina, I was on a bus traveling across the country from Córdoba to Mendoza when it dawned on me that I was hopelessly unprepared to speak to anybody in this vast and beautiful country of 24 million people. I listened to those around me and understood absolutely nothing. Argentines not only spoke rapidly, but also used words I never knew existed. What they said was just noise— at least to me. The only good thing to come from the twenty-hour bus ride was a simple but revelatory truth—after all my Spanish studying I had only the vocabulary of an Argentine pre-schooler. So guess whom I talked to for the first several months in the land of the *gauchos*? Children!

Talking to these children was not as bad as it sounds. They were actually quite patient with me and helped all they could. But I also learned to help myself. I decided as soon as I got off the bus in Mendoza that I was going to write down every word I heard that I didn't know, look it up in my pocket dictionary, and then write the word and its definition on a three-by-five-inch card. I carried this card with me all day and I would frequently pull it out and quiz myself. If we took a break during the day, I was mentally going over the list of that day's new words in my head. I listened to conversations and made an effort to use new words. At night, before going to sleep, I went through the entire list to make sure I had mastered all the vocabulary words.

Interestingly, I was not afraid to make a mistake or be corrected by a child or anyone else who knew what I didn't. This was new for me. My goal had become to learn—not to impress or avoid making a fool of myself. This certainly had not been my educational paradigm thus far! The significance of this tectonic shift in my thinking was not clear to me at the time, but it did become clear later.

Soon I found myself able to speak and understand conversational Spanish. The time actually arrived when I was able to go several days without having to write down a single word. My appetite had been whetted; I longed to learn more. So I started reading the New Testament in Spanish in the early morning. Same drill—find words I didn't know, look up their meaning, write them on my card and try to use them during the day. I studied these new words at every opportunity and continued to test myself at the end of each day.[9] After I finished the New Testament, I started reading the daily newspapers, and then it was on to high school textbooks on history and language all in Spanish. My vocabulary expanded exponentially. This went on every day of the week for the entire two years I was in Argentina.

My transition from talking to children to being able to speak coherently to educated adults was seamless and extraordinarily satisfying. In addition to working on my vocabulary, I spent countless hours studying and mastering Spanish grammar, as well as the correct accents for all the areas where I lived. By the time I left Argentina in December of 1970, I was fluent in Spanish and profoundly impressed with the country and her wonderful people.

But after returning home to Indio, California, I had no reason to continue increasing my Spanish vocabulary. I would start that habit again in a couple of months when I resumed my university studies at Brigham Young University, where I majored in Spanish. But soon after coming home, it hit me that increasing my vocabulary in English might not be a bad idea either. In day to day conversation, I never heard a word I didn't know. It was clear that I had to start to read if I wanted to expand my personal lexicon.

My mother recommended the first book I read after returning home from Argentina. It was a great novel written by the famous poet James Dickey. I read *Deliverance* in one sitting. It was that good. I was captivated by the story and the author's ability to put action into his words and thus make fiction come alive. The next book I read was Truman Capote's classic, *In Cold Blood*. I devoured Capote's masterpiece late one night—also in one sitting—finishing it by the early morning. Capote's descriptive gift was so remarkably real that I, a twenty-one-year-old man, not only could not fall asleep after finishing the book, but also had to keep the lights on. Read the following excerpt from Capote's book and you will understand why this is a one-sitting book and why it got me into reading great books:

> But then, in the earliest hours of that morning in No-
> vember, a Sunday morning, certain foreign sounds
> impinged on the normal nightly Holcomb noises—
> on the keening hysteria of coyotes, the dry scrape of
> scuttling tumbleweed, the racing, receding wail of lo-
> comotive whistles. At the time not a soul in sleeping
> Holcomb heard them—four shotgun blasts that, all
> told, ended six human lives. But afterward the towns-
> people, theretofore sufficiently unfearful of each other
> to seldom trouble to lock their doors, found fantasy
> re-creating them over and again—those somber ex-
> plosions that stimulated fires of mistrust in the glare
> of which many old neighbors viewed each other
> strangely, and as strangers.[10]

I don't recall the words I had to look up as I read either *In
Cold Blood* or *Deliverance*. But I am sure my love affair with
words and with the English language started with those two
books. When I moved into my current office in Palm Desert,
in 1998, I started to place books on my shelf in the order I
read them and then started to segregate them by year. From
1970 to 1998, I don't recall keeping track of the books I read
or the words I looked up; since then I have read over seven
hundred books. The book shelves at my office filled up long
ago and I have had to move many books to other locations.
As I read I highlighted words I didn't know in yellow and
wrote definitions for those words in the page margins. Many
of the words I looked up I wrote in a little black book that I
carried with me in my briefcase. If I thought the word had
been cleverly used in a sentence, I copied the entire sentence
down in my little black book. I frequently review this book
and quiz myself on the words and their meanings before re-
tiring to bed at night.

I went two decades without consciously making an effort to make sure I understood exactly what was being communicated to me, but it only took two years in a foreign country for me to open my eyes to the distinct disadvantage of a limited vocabulary. Once I understood the game, I started to play it with vigor. I didn't wait for a teacher to assign me a book or order me to open a dictionary. I started to study words on my own. I remember a trip my wife, Sue, and I made from Utah to California in 1972 when I was a senior in college. It was a ten-hour car trip so, as I drove, I had Sue go through a box that contained a thousand vocabulary words and quiz me on each one. Sue has the patience of Job, but I must say that drill was never again repeated in our thirty-seven years of marriage. Today it does not matter what I am reading; if I don't understand a word, I look it up. No exceptions! Today I don't circle the words that I know, e.g., "the" and "I"—I highlight the words I don't know and then look them up. It should be no surprise to anyone that my curiosity has increased as my understanding has deepened.

So what does my experience have to do with you?

It has to do with you because we probably share many things in common. Were you embarrassed as a child, either in church or in school, because you couldn't read or write or spell as well as the other kids? Did you have a teacher who assumed you knew what was going on so didn't really address the issues you needed to learn? Did you ever have an experience in school where you were absolutely overwhelmed by the amount of material that needed to be learned so you just simply decided it was better not to even make the effort? If you had any one or a combination of these things happen to you, then my experience in life and in learning will be of value to you.

To understand exactly what my life has to do with yours and why the message of my education is relevant to you, regardless of your age or your level of education, I think we need to turn to another book—one written by George Orwell and entitled *Nineteen Eighty-Four*.

I am not sure exactly when I read this classic, but I do know that the reading of it was what made me consciously realize and fully understand the compelling relationship between vocabulary and thought. Published the same year I was born—1949—*Nineteen Eighty-Four* is the story of Winston Smith and his struggle to survive in the world of Oceania where "BIG BROTHER IS WATCHING YOU." The book is fiction, thus the Orwellian world of Oceania does not exist, and for my purposes a complete explication of this literary masterpiece is not necessary. I only need to share with you the official language of Oceania—Newspeak—and describe how it came about and how it developed in order to make my point about the importance of one's vocabulary. Let me begin with the Appendix of the book—The Principles of Newspeak:

> Newspeak was the official language of Oceania and had been devised to meet the idealogical needs of Ingsoc, or English Socialism.[11]

> Quite apart from the suppression of definitely heretical words, reduction of vocabulary was regarded as an end in itself, and no word that could be dispensed with was allowed to survive. Newspeak was designed not to extend but to *diminish* the range of thought, and this purpose was indirectly assisted by cutting the choice of words down to a minimum....[12]

> Relative to our own, the Newspeak vocabulary was tiny, and new ways of reducing it were constantly being devised. Newspeak, indeed, differed from almost all other languages in that its vocabulary grew smaller instead of larger every year. Each reduction was a gain, since the smaller the area of choice, the smaller the temptation to take thought. Ultimately it was hoped to make articulate speech issue from the larynx without involv-

ing the higher brain centers at all....[13]

From the foregoing account it will be seen that in Newspeak the expression of unorthodox opinions, above a very low level, was well-nigh impossible.[14]

I am confident that *Nineteen Eighty-Four* was required reading at Indio High School when I was a student there in the 60s. Why I didn't read the book until a decade after high school is a mystery that I still can't fully explain. Probably I was just too lazy. When I finally got around to reading the book my first reaction was the usual: "Big Brother"—in other words, the government—is always watching you. Then I read the book again and an entirely different meaning became clear to me. If one really believes that "ignorance is strength"[15] then there is no better or straighter path to this ignorance than the elimination of words from one's vocabulary. Pay close attention to how the characters in George Orwell's novel make this point:

"How is the dictionary getting on?" said Winston, raising his voice to overcome the noise.

"Slowly," said Syme. "I'm on the adjectives. It's fascinating."...

"You think, I dare say, that our chief job is inventing new words. But not a bit of it! We're destroying words—scores of them, hundreds of them, every day. We're cutting the language down to the bone. The Eleventh Edition won't contain a single word that will become obsolete before the year 2050."[16]

"It's a beautiful thing, the destruction of words. It was B.B.'s idea originally, of course," he added as an afterthought.[17]

"Don't you see that the whole aim of Newspeak is to narrow the range of thought?...Every year fewer and fewer words, and the range of consciousness always a little smaller."[18]

I want to live in the United States of America, not Oceania. I look up words because I want to understand what people are trying to say to me, either verbally or in writing. I want to increase my cognitive ability and not allow my mind to atrophy.

Nobody who reads *Nineteen Eighty-Four* can help but be frightened by the effort of Oceania's government to control the thoughts of its citizens by limiting their vocabularies. Why then do we voluntarily limit our own vocabularies? Why do we ever stop looking up words? Why do we try to get by with the minimum? Are we embarrassed? Do we have a teacher who doesn't inspire or peers who make fun? Is it laziness, or do we find ignorance addictive? Maybe we just don't know what we are missing.

Let's get serious. If you are a high school student with an average IQ, you can go weeks without hearing a word you don't know. But try this experiment. Buy a copy of *The New Yorker* magazine and read it from cover to cover. The first time through don't look up any unfamiliar words—just skip them and figure out the meaning by context. Now re-read the magazine looking up all the words you do not know. Be honest with yourself. Did you really understand what the articles were trying to communicate when you did not know the meaning of all the words in them? I am sure you got the main points, but isn't it amazing what it is possible to miss the first time through?

One final word about words. A problem that I notice from time to time is what my brother Rick describes as "verbicide"—the deliberate distortion of the sense of a word. In this case, verbicide describes a phenomenon that occurs when certain words are routinely misused or overused. Let me give three examples: "enormity," "inflammable," and "awesome." Do you even really know what these words mean and, if so, when was the last time you heard them used correctly?

Many people, including newscasters and politicians, use

enormity when they are describing a place, an idea, or a very large problem (e.g., "The enormity of the Himalayas overwhelms the first time visitor."). Wrong! *The American Heritage Dictionary, Second College Edition* defines enormity as follows: "1. The quality of passing all moral bounds: excessive wickedness or outrageousness; 2. A monstrous offense or evil; outrage." (e.g., "The enormity of the Bataan Death March becomes clear when one learns that there was a dead body along the road every 30 ft. for 84 miles."). If you go to the trouble of looking up enormity in the dictionary, just scroll down one word and "enormousness"—the word which should be used to describe "very great in size, extent,"—jumps right out at you.

When was the last time you heard someone use the word "inflammable" to signify the opposite of "flammable?" Back to the dictionary—Inflammable "1. Tending to ignite easily and burn rapidly; flammable..." (*The American Heritage Dictionary, Second College Edition*) Flammable and inflammable mean the same thing.

We now turn from words that are frequently used incorrectly to a word that has been rendered useless by being used too frequently—"AWESOME" (inspiring awe). For example, I have lived for over fifty years and that word was seldom, if ever, a problem for me. Then suddenly it was there in almost every sentence I heard. The only great experiences anybody was having were "awesome" experiences. Every attractive man or woman was now "awesome." Every football, baseball, and basketball game was now "awesome" regardless of who won or lost. It didn't matter where you were, if you had ears you heard the word "awesome." "Awesome" was used to describe everything, so it eventually lost its meaning and now really describes nothing at all.

Spelling is an important aspect of vocabulary-building. In order to master a new word you need to learn how to spell it. I know this doesn't matter if you only plan on speaking, but from time to time we are called upon to write. My sister-in-law, Mavis, taught English to high school students in New Orleans when my brother Rick was in medical school. One day she came into the classroom and on the blackboard someone had written, "Clarence is a asho." In educational circles they call experiences like this "golden teaching moments." Seizing her "golden teaching moment," Mavis got busy and taught spelling for the next hour—and when to use "a" and when to use "an."

Rick is now a practicing dermatologist in Orem, Utah. He told me about tattoos he had recently seen that were memorable for their misspellings: One tattoo inked on a guy's suprapubic area reads: "My Branes are in my balls." Another literary classic was found on a bicep, and it read: "Brilance is my secret weapon."

It is one thing to misuse a word in speech; it is an entirely different message to permanently emboss a misspelled word on your arm or near your [expletive deleted].

CHAPTER 2

READING

It is almost unthinkable that, in such an abundant society, many adults cannot read. –Gordon B. Hinckley

The last book I read in Spanish was *The President's Plane is Missing*, by John J. Sterling. I read it in Argentina in 1970. I looked up every single word that was new to me and wrote it on a three-by-five-inch card, then memorized and incorporated these words into my working vocabulary. When I started to read novels in Spanish my motivation was to find new words, but to my surprise the reading experience was mind-expanding and enjoyable in itself. It made me curious. By the time I got on the airplane to return home, my educational paradigm had shifted from classroom learning to a daily life learning that was not only relevant, but also essential.

I returned to the United States in December of 1970, but I did not start school again until the end of January 1971. I had a month to kill, so I worked as a teaching assistant at the Coachella Valley High School in Thermal, California, and read at night for fun. Before this, when I sat down to read,

I had no direction or educational purpose other than to kill time and entertain myself. That all changed when I ran into Phil Ferranti, an old friend from school.

Phil Ferranti is a legend in the Coachella Valley. The son of a shoe salesman, he is an acknowledged boy-wonder genius who, after graduating from Indio High School, studied for the Catholic priesthood. Phil gave that up several years later and eventually became a teacher/counselor, then a writer and investment advisor. Phil is a very smart man—focused, educationally and intellectually oriented—and, as I was soon to find out, very well-read.

I have a clear memory of going to a bookstore in Palm Springs with Phil during this time and being hit between the eyes by a direct question he had asked me. The question changed my life. We were looking at the selection of books lined up against the wall and out of nowhere Phil asked me if I had read *The Grapes of Wrath* by John Steinbeck. I answered; "No." Phil didn't laugh or make a condescending comment—he just picked the book off the shelf and put it in my hands and said, "Jimmy, you have to read this!" Before we left the store that afternoon he had also given me *I and Thou* by Martin Buber, *Gift From the Sea* by Anne Morrow Lindbergh, and *Arrowsmith* by Sinclair Lewis.

I can't tell you exactly why I started to read them. Maybe I now understood what books could offer me and saw for the first time that I needed what was in them. Maybe I was just searching for more new words. But I didn't just start to read; I now read with a purpose. I read not only to increase my vocabulary but also to deepen my understanding of the world around me. I was supremely motivated.

I don't recall if Phil made a specific comment on the importance of reading or if he simply set an example for me. Either way, he made a significant impact. As I read the four books Phil had recommended, he and I would meet at my house and talk about them. We would go on and on for hours, late into the night, about the themes and ideas found within them. Phil liked Buber more than I did, but we both loved Steinbeck. As I listened to Phil talk, it became painfully clear that I had missed something important between kindergarten and twelfth grade. But before one month ended, I had undergone a life-altering paradigm shift in my thinking. I had become aware that Jim Parkinson was responsible for educating Jim Parkinson. And I also learned that reading was the most important way I could take charge of this education.

By the time I returned to Provo, Utah, to resume my university studies I had made the decision to read all of the American literary classics. I went to the Wilkinson Center Student Bookstore and started to buy them one at a time— *East of Eden* by John Steinbeck, *Main Street* by Sinclair Lewis, *The Jungle* by Upton Sinclair, *The Scarlet Letter* by Nathaniel Hawthorne, etc., and I bought them all in paperback. In one year I had read at least fifty of the most-admired books written by American authors. By the way, I continued to look up every word I didn't know and wrote the definition in the margin. I carried a paperback *American Heritage Dictionary* with me at all times.

As you undoubtedly noticed by the preceding paragraph, I went first to the fiction shelves to find my books. I loved involving myself in the lives of the characters: Tom Joad from the pages of *The Grapes of Wrath*, Pug Henry from *The Winds of War* and Atticus Finch from Harper Lee's classic *To Kill a Mockingbird*. Their lives were compelling. Literary themes are universal. I find it amazing that in the hands of a talented author, fiction can reveal as much truth, if not more, than historical works or biographies. I found, much to my surprise, the worst part about reading a great novel is that it ends.

My life went from dull to fascinating when I opened my eyes, opened a book, and opened my mind. As I began to read the American classics and look up words, I found myself thinking and talking more about ideas than people. This was a whole new world for me. The world of thoughts, concepts, and philosophies was soul-changing.

I chose books that I was interested in reading. This, in retrospect, was important. You cannot dictate to another person his/her literary taste. Please do not try. Either something intrigues you or it doesn't. Interest cannot be manufactured, but it can be guided. Phil Ferranti not only directed my reading, but he also encouraged it. I found his intellect seductive. I subconsciously wanted to be as smart and as well-read, so for a season I read what he read and/or suggested.

I also found a lot of time in which I could do my reading. I would read for fifteen to thirty minutes in the morning before I went to class. I read in those few minutes before class while I waited for the professor to begin. I read as I ate lunch. I read after I studied and before I went to sleep at night, and none of the books were assigned reading for any of the classes I was taking.

Years later I found the book *The Rise of Theodore Roosevelt* by Edmund Morris and learned that I was certainly not the only person who had read in his spare time. President Roosevelt was a voracious reader who made time to read even during the presidential campaign of 1900. On page 730 of Morris's extraordinary biography we find the diary entry of a presidential aide who set out a "timetable of one undated campaign day":

7:00 a.m.	Breakfast
7:30 a.m.	A speech
8:00 a.m.	*Reading a historical work*
9:00 a.m.	A speech
10:00 a.m.	Dictating letters
11:00 a.m.	Discussing Montana mines
11:30 a.m.	A speech
12:00	*Reading an ornithological work*
12:30 p.m.	A speech
1:00 p.m.	Lunch
1:30 p.m.	A speech
2:30 p.m.	*Reading Sir Walter Scott*
3:00 p.m.	Answering telegrams
3:45 p.m.	A speech
4:00 p.m.	Meeting the press
4:30 p.m.	*Reading*
5:00 p.m.	A speech
6:00 p.m.	*Reading*
7:00 p.m.	Supper
8-10 p.m.	Speaking
11:00 p.m.	*Reading alone in his car*
12:00	To bed.[19]

I do not recall when my interest shifted from fiction to non-fiction, but now I read mostly biographies, autobiographies, and history books. I guess my interests have changed in part because I am at heart a history *aficionado*—if I wasn't *there*, I want to at least know what happened *there*. I am also fascinated by how great people become great. How others handle fear, fortune and crisis is extremely interesting to me as well as instructive.

Have you ever seen a jigsaw puzzle that didn't have the picture of the puzzle on the box? Why do we need to know what the puzzle is supposed to look like before we start to assemble it? Why is the motto of The 100 Black Men of America—"What you see is what you will be"? The answer to these questions is evident. Do you want a template for living a successful life? Read the biography or autobiography of a great man or woman. Avoid the silly, poorly written autobiographies. Rather, focus on books that speak truth about real people who overcame fears, shortcomings, and mistakes— Eleanor Roosevelt, Abraham Lincoln, and Nelson Mandela jumped into the arena of life, where they all soared and plummeted. Reading about Roosevelt, Lincoln, and Mandela gave me an appreciation for history and inspired me with personal character traits that I could both admire and emulate.

During my lifetime, I have read literally hundreds of biographies and autobiographies, and the protagonist's love of reading is a common thread that unites them all.

We learn of Benjamin Franklin's devotion to literature in his autobiography:

> From a child I was fond of reading, and all the little money that came into my hands was ever laid out in books.[20]

Another writer whose works I have enjoyed over the years is Sinclair Lewis. His *Arrowsmith* was one of the first books I read. That was in 1971. Since that time I have read: *Main Street, Dodsworth, Elmer Gantry,* and *Babbit.* In his book on Lewis, *Sinclair Lewis: Rebel From Main Street,* Richard Lingeman, referring to Sinclair as Harry, writes the following:

> Harry's imagination was fed by his voracious reading. His father had books, but the boy soon ran through them and foraged in the public library. The town legend arose that by the time he went

to college he had read every book on its shelves. From his reading and his father's repeated admonitions to look up words he
didn't know, he developed a precocious vocabulary. 'Harry musta
swallowed the dictionary!' boys taunted. Another contemporary
remembered him as a know-it-all who chattered on about some
subject until others were bored; he seemed only to care about
what *he* was interested in. But he thought what was fascinating to
him should be fascinating to others....[21]

Now I would like to focus on two of the most influential
and important men in the history of the English-speaking
world: Winston Churchill and Abraham Lincoln. Although
born into a family of privilege, Winston Churchill was not
expected to become a great man. As a matter of fact, Winston's father, Randolph Churchill, said of his son that "he
would have to go for a soldier, that he was too stupid for anything else."[22] How did a young man who was thought "too
stupid" by his own father go on to become one of the most
important statesmen of the twentieth century? The following
quotes from William Manchester's The Last Lion give us a
partial understanding of this remarkable man's development:

> At Harrow his lifelong fascination with words grew. He was thir-
> teen, and Somervell was introducing him to literature...Winston
> was soon deep in Thackeray, Dickens, Wordsworth, and every
> biography he could lay his hands on...Inevitably his vocabulary
> increased...The bookseller Moore, who saw him almost daily,
> noticed that he was displaying 'evidences of his unusual com-
> mand of words. He would argue in the shop on any subject, and,
> as a result of this, he was, I am afraid, often left in sole posses-
> sion of the floor.' At this point another teacher, L. M. Moriarty,
> Winston's fencing master, suggested that he drop in on him eve-
> nings at home to discuss essays and history. They talked, not only
> of content, but also of form, particularly essay techniques then
> being developed by Stevenson, Ruskin, Huxley, and Cardinal
> Newman. **None of this was reflected in the report cards sent to
> Connaught Place, but the autodidactic pattern was forming.
> Winston was being taught to teach himself. He would always
> be a dud in the classroom and a failure in examinations, but
> in his own time, on his own terms, he would become one of**

the most learned statesmen of the coming century [emphasis added].[23]

Perhaps the following examples of Churchill at his rhetorical best inform the reader why this "child who was too stupid" became the man whose voice and speeches helped save the free world. On page 6 of William Manchester's *The Last Lion: Visions of Glory, 1874–1932*, we read:

> If this long island story of ours is to end at last, let it end only when each one of us lies choking in his own blood upon the ground...'I have nothing to offer but blood, toil, tears, and sweat....

> Even though large tracts of Europe and many old and famous states have fallen or may fall into the grip of the Gestapo and all the odious apparatus of Nazi rule, we shall not flag or fail. We shall go on to the end. We shall fight in France, we shall fight on the seas and oceans, we shall fight with growing confidence and growing strength in the air, we shall defend our island, whatever the cost may be, we shall fight on the beaches, we shall fight on the landing grounds, we shall fight in the fields and in the streets, we shall fight in the hills; we shall never surrender....

> "Behind us," he said, "...gather a group of shattered states and bludgeoned races: the Czechs, the Poles, the Danes, the Norwegians, the Belgians, the Dutch—upon all of whom a long night of barbarism will descend, unbroken even by a star of hope, unless we conquer, as conquer we must, as conquer we shall"..."This England never did, nor never shall, / Lie at the proud foot of a conqueror."[24]

It should surprise no one that the man who said, "It was the nation and the race dwelling all round the globe that had the lion's heart; I had the luck to be called upon to give the roar," loved books and wrote this of them:

> If you cannot read all your books, at any rate handle, or, as it were, fondle them—peer into them, let them fall open where they will, read from the first sentence that arrests the eye, set them back on their shelves with your own hands, arrange them on your own plan so that if you do not know what is in them, you will at least know where they are. Let them be your friends; let them at any rate be your acquaintances.[25]

Winston Churchill was a towering figure in the twentieth century and is considered by most historians to be the most important statesman of that time. He was not only the Prime Minister of Great Britain during World War II; he was also the voice that saved the free world. It was his leadership and his rhetorical skill that rallied the Allies to fight back the evil of Nazi Germany and preserve our democratic way of life.

Over the years I have read numerous works on Abraham Lincoln but *Lincoln,* David Donald's biography, is probably the best book I have ever read on the life of the sixteenth president. Recently, however, I came across a new book by Fred Kaplan, *Lincoln: The Biography of a Writer,* which I consider to be a must-read for anyone who wants to understand how Lincoln became Lincoln. I will share a few quotes:

> He read and reread as much as time and his few books allowed...[26]

> The autodidact was about to become immersed in new reading experiences. Previously limited to the Bible and *Dilworth's Speller,* he now also got editions of Aesop's fables and John Bunyan's seventeenth-century Puritan allegory, *Pilgrim's Progress*...[27]

> He 'would go out in the woods & gather hickory bark—bring it home & Keep a light by it and read by it—when no lamp was to be had—grease lamp—handle to it which Stuck in the crack of the wall.'...[28]

> But he read whenever and wherever he could. 'Abe was not Energetic Except in one thing,' his newly arrived half-sister Matilda remarked, 'he was active & persistant [sic] in learning—read Everything he Could.' He 'devoured all the books he could get or lay hands on; he was a Constant and voracious reader,' John Hanks noticed. 'When he went out to work any where he would Carry his books and would always read while resting,' a friend recalled...[29]

> ...he had a passion for reading, which he now directed toward the borrowed law books he was determined to master...He spent much time reading a volume of Shakespeare, which he carried

with him...[30]

If Lincoln "rose" on a tide of literacy, he took America with him. Mr. Lincoln's extraordinary ability to articulate the zeitgeist of nineteenth century America can only be explained and understood in the context of his exposure to the great thinkers and writers who preceded him. The following quotes from his First Inaugural, Second Inaugural and Gettysburg Addresses, respectively, give a glimpse into Lincoln's staggering genius:

> ...I am loathe to close. We are not enemies, but friends. We must not be enemies. Though passion may have strained, it must not break our bonds of affection. The mystic chords of memory, stretching from every battlefield, and patriot grave, to every living heart and hearth-stone, all over this broad land, will yet swell the chorus of the Union, when again touched, as surely they will be, by the better angels of our nature. (First Inaugural Address, March 4, 1861).

> ...With malice toward none, with charity for all with firmness in the right as God gives us to see the right, let us strive on to finish the work we are in, to bind up the nation's wounds, to care for him who shall have borne the battle and for his widow and his orphan, to do all which may achieve and cherish a just and lasting peace among ourselves and with all nations. (Second Inaugural Address, March 4, 1865).

> ...But, in a larger sense, we cannot dedicate—we cannot consecrate—we cannot hallow—this ground. The brave men, living and dead, who struggled here have consecrated it, far above our poor power to add or detract. The world will little note, nor long remember, what we say here, but it can never forget what they did here. (Gettysburg Address, November 19, 1863).

Abraham Lincoln saved the Union, and it would be hard to find a history student in America who could not recite from memory a few lines of his Gettysburg Address. The president who freed the slaves simultaneously emancipated the greatest democracy the world has ever known. Abraham Lincoln was as skillful with the English language as Winston

Churchill was.

What gives birth to a Winston Churchill or an Abraham Lincoln? Were both these men preordained or foreordained to greatness? Not really. One was thought too stupid, and the other emerged from the backwoods of Kentucky with little or no formal education. Undoubtedly, many divergent factors and experiences contributed to making Churchill and Lincoln into singular historical figures, and there can be no question that there was something intrinsically special about them. But history is clear in pointing out that they both took responsibility for their own educations; in a word, they were autodidacts.

I heartily agree with the historian Arthur M. Schlesinger, who wrote, "Biography offers an easy education in American history, rendering the past more human, more vivid, more intimate, more accessible, more connected to ourselves." Autobiographies, biographies and books about history are interesting and entertaining. Emerson is also right: "There is properly no history; only biography." Still, no matter into which century my reading takes me, I'm living my life in the present and I have to remember that and keep things real.

I know I will never become a Winston Churchill or an Abraham Lincoln, but their stories and their lives have become an important part of my life and have helped shape my character and my career. To be a better, more effective me, I have taken a page from their histories and in particular, like them, I have taken responsibility for my own education. And so should you. Do not let the Randolph Churchills in your family dictate what you will become. Do not let a teacher or a peer embarrass or discourage you into educational paralysis.

I treasure the past and recognize its importance. That is

partly why I read biographies and books on history. On the facade of the building housing the national archives in Washington, D.C., is found the quote "Past is Prologue." George Santayana once said, "Those who cannot remember the past are condemned to repeat it." I want to make correct decisions and avoid the consequences of bad decisions. Instead of repeating the mistakes of those who have preceded me, I want their lives to give direction to mine. How better to learn the lessons of yesterday than by reading about them today.

History enlightens the past and illuminates the future. History gives context and meaning to the continuum of the human experiment. Without it, we begin the world anew every generation. Without the torch of history to give the outline of the path that lies ahead, we are destined to blindly stumble our way to the grave. We shouldn't just leave history in history books; we should dig deep into it, so that the past can help us frame current events and give hope and direction to our future.

In churches across America, preachers warn that the world has never been so evil, and, because of our collective and personal corruption, the end of the world is near. There is no denying that some horrible people are doing some remarkably ugly and destructive things today, but hasn't the world seen this before? Before the next Sabbath I suggest that men and women of the cloth get a copy of William Manchester's book *A World Lit Only by Fire: The Medieval Mind and the Renaissance: Portrait of an Age*, and read all 322 of its pages. Then, they should go to a bookstore and buy any work dedicated to a discussion of the Holocaust and to those who conceived and implemented that genocide. They should force themselves to read every word and emotionally come to grips with that dark chapter in the book of past human evil. Knowing history keeps us from arriving at inaccurate conclusions and silly and dangerous public policies. Whether we learn the lessons of what has passed and make the world a better place depends on if, and when, we learn that the "only thing new in the world is the history we don't know."

I am not sure we have learned the lessons of history. Are there Abraham Lincolns and Winston Churchills working their way through our American educational system today, learning new words and reading every chance they get? Possibly. But my experience traveling the country these last few years makes me a little nervous about this. Let me explain.

With Lee Benson I wrote a book several years ago entitled *Soldier Slaves: Abandoned by the White House, Courts, and Congress.* To help promote the book, and also basic literacy in our high schools, I developed a program using *Soldier Slaves* as a text to teach history, politics, and law. I called the program "Literacy for the 21st Century." In the first forty-five minutes I talk about World War II, history, politics, and law as discussed in my book. The second forty-five minutes are dedicated to literacy.

To make the literacy program interactive, I ask the teacher for a list of the three smartest kids in the class. I ask these kids to come to the front of the classroom to help me with my presentation. When the students are in front of the white board I ask them the following question: "What is our national anthem?" Then I have one of the students write "The Star-Spangled Banner" on the board. You guessed it, more than half the time the student helpers leave out the hyphen between "Star" and "Spangled." I then ask a student, "What is a star?" One hundred percent of the time they get that right. They also answer the next question right: "What is a banner?" The question that has stumped over three thousand high school students from California to Utah, and from New Jersey to Mississippi is, "What does 'spangled' mean?" According to *The American Heritage Dictionary, Second College Edition,* spangled means "to adorn or cause to sparkle by covering with or as if with spangles. (A small, often circular piece of sparkling metal or plastic sewn especially on garments for decorations)." I've only had three answer that question correctly in the three years I've asked it. I was discouraged with our children until I asked a college-educated adult at a dinner party what "spangled" meant and she didn't know! I then became worried about America.

"You have got to be kidding," I thought. We hear the National Anthem before every sporting event played in this country. We memorize the words as children and sing the song in elementary school. We know the title, but we are never curious enough to grab a dictionary to look up the one word in the title we don't know. Can you say "incurious?" That word describes the cancer that has metastasized and now threatens to destroy young people in America.

By the time I finish my presentation to the high school class, I want every student to understand how important literacy is and how relevant knowing how to read and write is to success in life. I know that many who sit in the classroom and listen to me are behind in their education and are too embarrassed or too proud to ask for help. Maybe they don't even know they need it. Maybe they don't care. To help these children I share the following stories because they inspired me and they give hope to anyone who has the desire to better him or herself.

‹❦›

Frederick Douglass was an American slave born around 1820 in Maryland. Mr. Douglass, like most other slaves of his time, had "no accurate knowledge of [his] age, never having seen any authentic record containing it." I didn't really know that much about Frederick Douglass and his remarkable struggle to make a life for himself until I read his autobiography. No matter how disadvantaged the student sitting in a classroom in America, he or she does not face the challenges which Mr. Douglass faced and overcame. On page 44 of the *Narrative of the Life of Frederick Douglass*, we find the key to his success:

> Very soon after I went to live with Mr. and Mrs. Auld, she very kindly commenced to teach me the A, B, C. After I had learned this, she assisted me in learning to spell words of three or four letters. Just at this point of my progress, Mr. Auld found out what was going on, and at once forbade Mrs. Auld to instruct me further, telling her, among other things, that it was unlawful, as well as unsafe, to teach a slave to read. To use his own words, further, he said, 'If you give a nigger an inch, he will take an ell. A nigger should know nothing but to obey his master—to do as he is told to do. Learning would *spoil* the best nigger in the world. Now," said he, "if you teach that nigger (speaking of myself) how to read, there would be no keeping him. It would forever unfit him to be a slave. He would at once become unmanageable, and of no value to his master. As to himself, it could do him no good, but a great deal of harm. It would make him discontented and unhappy.' These words sank deep into my heart, stirred up sentiments within that lay slumbering, and called into existence an entirely new train of thought. It was a new and special revelation, explaining dark and mysterious things, with which my youthful understanding had struggled, but struggled in vain. I now understood what had been to me a most perplexing difficulty—to wit, the white man's power to enslave the black man. It was a grand achievement, and I prized it highly. From that moment, I understood the pathway from slavery to freedom. It was just what I wanted, and I got it at a time when I least expected it. Whilst I was saddened by the thought of losing the aid of my kind mistress, I was gladdened by the invaluable instruction which, by the merest accident, I had gained from my master. Though conscious

of the difficulty of learning without a teacher, I set out with high hope, and a fixed purpose, at whatever cost of trouble, to learn how to read.[31]

Students searching for a more current example of an autodidact who played a major role on the world stage, need look no further than these excerpts from *The Autobiography of Malcolm X*. On page 198-199 we read:

> Many who today hear me somewhere in person, or on television, or those who read something I've said, will think I went to school far beyond the eighth grade. This impression is due entirely to my prison studies.

> It had really begun back in the Charlestown Prison, when Bimbi first made me feel envy of his stock of knowledge. Bimbi had always taken charge of any conversation he was in, and I had tried to emulate him. But every book I picked up had few sentences which didn't contain anywhere from one to nearly all of the words that might as well have been in Chinese. When I just skipped those words, of course, I really ended up with little idea of what the book said. So I had come to the Norfolk Prison Colony still going through only book-reading motions. Pretty soon, I would have quit even these motions, unless I had received the motivation that I did.

> I have often reflected upon the new vistas that reading opened to me. I knew right there in prison that reading had changed forever the course of my life. As I see it today, the ability to read awoke inside me some long dormant craving to be mentally alive. I certainly wasn't seeking any degree, the way a college confers a status symbol upon its students. My homemade education gave me, with every additional book that I read, a little bit more sensitivity to the deafness, dumbness, and blindness that was afflicting the black race in America. Not long ago, an English writer telephoned me from London, asking questions. One was, "What's your alma mater?" I told him, "Books...."[32]

As I gathered information for this book and organized quotes that I thought would be helpful to the reader, I decided to take a fact-finding field trip. I was interested in finding out why some men fail in life and others succeed. What better place to study failure than in prison? So I made arrangements through Steve Killpack, a friend of mine who is the federal defender in Utah, to visit the Utah State Prison in Draper, Utah.

This prison visit was enlightening. According to Warden Steven Turley, the inmates are tested when they arrive and only about 45 percent of them are found to be literate. No wonder these men can't find jobs. They lacked the necessary skills to earn a legitimate living in today's society.

I met with four prisoners in a small room—without guards—and interviewed them for about two hours. Warden Turley warned me not to use three words with the prisoners unless I was prepared to have a fight break out: punk, bitch, and lame. Vocabulary words even matter behind bars! Only one of the prisoners had graduated from high school but told me, "I didn't learn anything." Only one said he could read—but based on the way he talked I don't think he was really telling the truth. In school they were all made fun of because they were illiterate—"I just beat the hell out of those who made fun of me!" I told them about my Literacy for the 21st Century program and asked them for advice on what I could say to high school students in order to motivate them to read. One of the inmates shared his life story with me. Halfway through it he began to cry. "I know I am somebody!...I chose the wrong path. Tell them it is up to them to choose the right path." My brother-in-law, Dr. David Greene, is a PhD who has dedicated his life to working with prison inmates. I spoke to him about what I had learned in the prison in Utah, and David told me that illiteracy is a universal problem among non-white-collar criminals.

When I first thought about writing this book I thought I knew exactly who my audience would be—young boys and girls between the ages of fourteen and eighteen. Now that

I have finished the book I've seen my target expand. If you are interested in living a full life—you are my audience. If you want a job—you are my audience. If you are a parent and you take your responsibilities for raising your children seriously—you are my audience. Learning how to read is as important in the twenty-first century as is breathing. If you don't have a good vocabulary, your reading will be limited. If you don't read, you cannot write. However, if you embrace education as a "personal responsibility" and diligently and doggedly pursue your lifetime goals, you will increase your chances of success exponentially and will savor the sweetness of knowing that you, and not your circumstances, control your future.

CHAPTER 3

WRITING

That's not writing ... that's typing. –Truman Capote

Several years ago I was in my garage and came across a briefcase I hadn't opened in years. In it I was pleased and surprised to find photographs that had been taken over forty years ago. Unfortunately, I also found a bundle of letters held together with a rubber band that I had written to my mother while I was serving as a Mormon missionary in Argentina. Today I pride myself on being a wordsmith who, since birth, has been writing memorable prose and poetry. Those long-forgotten letters put the lie to that myth. As I sat down and began to read them I became re-acquainted with a remarkably undereducated illiterate who produced an awkward series of forgettable sentences that were few in number and bereft of serious content. That person was me. I was so horrified that I threw the letters away.

How did I get from there to here? How did I ever become a serious, published writer?

I don't recall learning anything about the art of writing

until my freshman year in college. The class was English I, but I wasn't learning a thing from the class or from the teacher. Every Monday we were assigned an essay that had to be written and turned in by Friday. For the first time in my life I decided to actually sit down, think through the assignment, and make an effort to write something I would be proud of. Fortunately, in the fall of 1967, I had met a beautiful sophomore girl from San Francisco who turned out to be not only a grammar wiz who knew how to edit, but also was someone who found me cute. Sue Greene became my first editor, my best friend, and my severest critic—and eventually she also became my wife.

I later learned that editing my freshman papers was not the highlight of Sue's second year in college. My spelling was horrible and my sentence structures were so bad they literally collapsed under the weight of her heavy editing pen. After spending a great deal of time deciphering my penmanship, she cleaned up my literary messes, put the words in their correct order, shuffled the paragraphs and typed my papers. I put my name on them and I turned them in. The stories were based on my ideas, after all, so I felt no shame in taking full credit and allowing the "A" to be put on my transcript.

Soon, Sue and I had worked out a rather interesting arrangement. After I would receive my assignment on Monday, I would work on it all week and then on Thursday night I would meet Sue on the first floor of "S" Hall, one of the men's dormitory towers at Brigham Young University, and go over my paper with her before she put it in final form and typed it. Sue would patiently work through each paragraph and ask me, "What exactly are you trying to say?" We would talk through my point until my thinking was clear and my thought process logical. I should add here that Sue is Teutonic and so logic is second nature to her. Not until the ideas were clear were they allowed to flow out of the pen and go down on the paper. By the end of the year, the light had finally gone on in my head—the first rule of good writing is clear thinking. Thank you, Sue!

When Sue came across a punctuation error I had made, she would stop and point it out to me. When the sentences didn't flow, Sue would not gloss over them. She taught me why what I had written was wrong and how it needed to be changed. I listened and learned.

Becoming acquainted with good writing made me intolerant of sloppy prose and poor grammar. But as the mission letters to my mother attest, without Sue's constant, weekly encouragement, it didn't take long for me to fall back into bad habits. One school year is not long enough to make a writer. I found out over the next forty years that perfecting "the writing craft" takes enormous effort, dedication, and time.

Let's start at the beginning. Why don't we enjoy writing memos, letters, or anything else, for that matter? Because writing takes time. It takes time to craft a sentence. It is much easier to pick up the cell phone and tell somebody what you are thinking than it is to block out time to sit in front of a computer and map it out. Talking is a lot easier than writing—you really don't have to think before you speak. If you don't believe me, spend a day listening and keep a record of all the profound comments you heard in casual conversation. If you hear even one during the day I would be surprised. Speaking does not necessarily expose illogical and poorly thought-out concepts and ideas, but writing does. The very act of writing requires thinking. If a thought is not clear in the head, it will never be clear on the computer screen. Once you

see an idea written down that is poorly thought-out or illogical, the error becomes glaringly apparent and you are forced
to re-think your idea or concept and work it until it becomes
intelligible. Pride compels you, if nothing else. That's why we
avoid writing; we are intellectually lazy.

There is no way around it—if you want to learn how to
be a writer you have to write and you have to be prepared to
make mistakes and correct them. You have to grow a thick
skin so when someone else edits your work you will not be
too proud to simply tear it up, throw it away and begin again.
I learned this lesson the hard way. Prior to leaving for my
mission in Argentina, I spent one week in the mission home
in Salt Lake City, Utah. Upon first entering the mission home
all the missionaries were told to keep a journal. We were told
that it was important that we "write down our thoughts."

Every night at about 11:00 p.m. I sat quietly on my bed,
composed my ideas and then wrote them down in a little
black missionary journal. I wrote in my journal religiously
four days in a row. On the fifth day, I made the mistake of going back and reading what I had written. What I had written
could generously be described as the inchoate ramblings of
a non-reflective, remarkably immature simpleton. And that's
being very kind. I was not just embarrassed, I was humiliated
by what I had written—so much so that I immediately threw
my journal away and only wrote poorly constructed letters to
my mother for the next two years.

When I returned to college in 1971 and resumed my university studies, I knew the time had arrived for me to become
a serious student. Grades became very important to me and
I understood what I had to do to get them. Why did I become a better writer? I became a better writer for one simple
reason—I had to write better in order to get good grades.

How did I become a better writer and get better grades? I now took the time to think before I wrote and I also carefully edited all of my work before I turned in my papers; and most importantly, because of my hard work with vocabulary and reading, I now had a solid foundation. I had read enough to at least know what good writing was, and I had the words in my head to make original ideas and complex concepts possible. To borrow a metaphor from Stephen King, "I now had the tools in my toolbox," making it possible for me to accurately describe in words what I was thinking and feeling. That I could write for fun and personal satisfaction didn't occur to me until after I had graduated from law school and had worked as a trial lawyer for many years.

It was a case I was handling and an experience I had with a client that got me to write something that I didn't have to turn in to a teacher or submit to a judge. The client's name was Marciano Guzman and my experience with him was soul-altering.

~~~

MARCIANO GUZMAN

My father never allowed me to operate any type of machinery. Since dad considered a lawnmower a machine, I never complained. Mowing the lawn in Indio, California, during the month of August, when temperatures frequently hit one hundred ten degrees, was not a job I really wanted. My father was raised on a farm in southern Idaho and knew first hand just how dangerous equipment with moving parts could be. I don't know where Marciano Guzman's father was raised, but apparently he didn't care what kind of equipment his son worked on. Or maybe the family just needed the money.

Marciano Guzman was only sixteen years old when the accident occurred. It was a school night; it was late. He should have been home in bed, but he was working. In the Coachella Valley, when it's harvest time there is work in the fields twenty-four hours a day, seven days a week. Anybody who wanted to work had a job. Since he was a boy, Marciano was assigned the worst, and also the most dangerous, job.

A carrot harvesting machine has many moving parts and is as large as an eighteen-wheeler. The machine not only picks carrots from the ground but it also cuts the tops off these carrots and then hauls them up a conveyor belt that eventually dumps them into a truck that is positioned adjacent to the harvester. After being severed from the carrots, the tops simply fall to the ground. In theory, all moving parts on the machine are to be covered by a non-removable guard. The working reality dictates that the guard covering the sprocket on the conveyor belt taking the picked carrots to the adjacent truck be removed. Wet carrot tops frequently get stuck in the sprocket, and to avoid shutting down the entire machine, a worker stands right next to the conveyor belt, and as the carrot tops get stuck, he frees them with a sawed-off-broomstick. This cannot be done if the guard is in place. Removing the clogged carrot tops from the conveyor belt chain was Marciano's job on the night he got hurt.

The only light illuminating the machine that night came from a single bulb hanging from the top of the machine. Marciano couldn't see well in the dark, but he had done this job before and he was young and unafraid.

No one heard Marciano's scream as his worn tennis shoe slipped on the wet surface. His right arm became trapped, and then pulled by the moving chain into the sprocket. The machine was on and the boy's painful cry was drowned out by the continuous sound of the conveyor taking carrots up to the truck. It was harvest season and time was money. The fall was sudden, and the injury so traumatic it would be another twenty-four hours before Marciano realized his right arm was gone.

If that same accident happened today, Marciano Guzman would be limited to workman's compensation benefits only. Fortunately, back in the early eighties Marciano could sue his employer directly, under the doctrine of peculiar risk. I represented Marciano and we won, but the defendants appealed the jury's verdict. It was while we were waiting for the appellate court to decide if we were going to be able to keep the verdict, that I learned who the Savior was referring to when he said in Matthew 25:40:

> ...Verily I say unto you, Inasmuch as ye have done it unto one of the least of these my brethren, ye have done it unto me.

At the time I tried the Guzman case I was an associate in the law offices of Thomas T. Anderson in Indio, California. As one entered our offices, there was a long hall that led to the receptionist's desk. On the north and south sides of the waiting room there were two beautiful gardens. My private office faced the north garden and when I left the shutters open I could see the clients as they entered the reception area.

While we were waiting for the appellate court to decide our case, Marciano would frequently stop by the office to visit—always unannounced and never with an appointment. He was upbeat and fun to talk to, so most of the time I was glad to see him—but not always.

Even though I have a remarkably good memory, I cannot recall what was bothering me that particular day. But I was in a horrible mood. I must have been under a lot of pressure. Whatever the reason, I was actually feeling sorry for myself, and contrary to my gregarious personality, I wanted to be alone, finish the day's work, and go home. Fortunately, I had rarely felt that way before or since. In the middle of that down day I looked up from my work and saw Marciano enter the reception area and take a seat. I knew why he was there. No appointment; he just showed up because he was lonely and wanted to talk to someone. I was alone in my office, but I was not lonely, and because I was having "one of those days," I sure as hell didn't want to talk to anybody. My insensitivity was out of character. I invited my client into my office and tried my best to act interested; I failed.

Marciano may have lost his right arm but his intuition was still intact. He immediately sensed that I was different. He tried to make jokes and tease, but I didn't really respond. Our conversation was a long silence interrupted by meaningless stares. Finally he just came out with it: "Mr. Parkinson, something is wrong. You are acting funny, are you all right?" I decided just to tell him the truth.

I forgot I was with a young man who was missing his right arm. I didn't want to go into detail but I began slowly. I explained how busy I was and the enormous pressure I was working under. I tried to explain my depression and my bad mood. Marciano was stunned. "How can you be having a bad day...you have a family...a beautiful wife...kids...everybody knows you are the baddest lawyer in the valley...and you drive a f***ing Mercedes Benz...are you crazy?"

"Marciano, I hate to break the news to you, but even I can have a bad day." I will never forget what happened next.

Marciano got up and said, "I guess I better leave you alone to do your s***." He then started to open my office door to leave, but something stopped him. He paused, turned around, looked me in the eye and said, "Would it help if I gave you a hug?"

Now I was stunned. I didn't answer out loud; I simply nodded my head.

We walked toward each other and met in the middle of my office. We said nothing. Then a farm boy not yet twenty years old wrapped his left arm around his lawyer and hugged him. Neither one of us spoke. Marciano opened the door and left my office. I watched him walk down the hall and disappear. Returning to my desk, "the least of these my brethren" sat down in his oversized chair, placed his head in his hands, and quietly wept.*

Before concluding this chapter on writing, there are a couple of other thoughts I would like to share. Over the last ten years as I have read, I have tried to select books that were interesting and well-written. Some people browse bookstores and buy books based on the cover. I, on the other hand, always open them up and read the first paragraph. If it's not well written I won't buy it. Let me give you some memorable opening sentences:

> Sinclair Lewis introduces the main character in the first sentence in *Elmer Gantry* as follows: "Elmer Gantry was drunk."
>
> Ayn Rand's famous opening sentence to her epic novel, *The Fountainhead*, reads, "Howard Roark laughed."

---

* The California Court of Appeal, Fourth District, Division Two affirmed the jury's verdict...Marciano won!

For pure genius consider Leo Tolstoy's opening to *Anna Karenina*: "All happy families resemble one another, each unhappy family is unhappy in its own way."

The answer—at least for me—is that these opening sentences caught my attention and enticed me to keep reading. I wanted to know who Elmer Gantry and Howard Roark were and why was Elmer drunk and Howard laughing. I also wanted to know if Tolstoy could write another sentence in his 963-page masterpiece that would equal his opening line for profundity and literary brilliance. Read the books. Now let's read some opening paragraphs. It is hard to find a better non-fiction writer than Rick Atkinson. This is how he begins his book, *An Army at Dawn*:

> Twenty-seven acres of headstones fill the American cemetery at Carthage, Tunisia. There are no obelisks, no tombs, no ostentatious monuments, just 2,841 bone-white marble markers, two feet high and arrayed in ranks as straight as gunshots. Only the chiseled names and dates of death suggest singularity. Four sets of brothers lie side by side. Some 240 stones are inscribed with thirteen of the saddest words in our language: "Here rests in honored glory a comrade in arms known but to God." A long limestone wall contains the names of another 3,724 men still missing, and a benediction: "Into Thy hands, O Lord."[33]

Another example of great writing is found in the first paragraph of Timothy B. Tyson's remarkable memoir *Blood Done Sign My Name*:

> "Daddy and Roger and 'em shot 'em a *nigger*." That's what Gerald Teel said to me in my family's driveway in Oxford, North Carolina, on May 12, 1970. We were both ten years old. I was bouncing a basketball. The night before, a black man had 'said something' at the store to Judy, his nineteen-year-old sister-in-law, Gerald told me, and his father and two of his brothers had run him out of the store and shot him dead. The man's name was Henry Marrow, I found out later, but his family called him Dickie. He was killed in public as he lay on his back, helpless, begging for his life.[34]

Great paragraphs begin with great sentences. Great sentences are made up of descriptive words cobbled together by thought and purpose and then powerfully ordered. The whole process begins with a thought or an event, and punctuation keeps the thoughts from running over events.

Let's talk seriously for a moment about the importance of punctuation. Over the years I have read and relied on books that deal with common errors in the English language. Some I like are: *The Most Common Errors in English Usage and How to Avoid Them, Learn How to Control Grammar Rather Than Letting it Control You,* by Elaine Bender; *Grammar Girls, Quick and Dirty Tips for Better Writing,* by Mignon Fogarty; and also, *Powerful Writing Skills,* by Rich Andersen. I have also read and used *Writing with Style, Conversations on the Art of Writing,* by John R. Trimble. By far, the best book I have read on punctuation is *Eats, Shoots and Leaves,* by Lynne Truss. Two sentences from her book—made up of the same seven words in exactly the same order, but punctuated differently—make it abundantly clear just how important correct punctuation is to meaning:

A woman, without her man, is nothing.

A woman: without her, man is nothing.

Read these two sentences out loud and when you read, follow the instructions of the punctuation. By reading out loud and following the given punctuation, the meaning becomes clear. Obviously, punctuation matters!

Although I have mentioned it before—the point bears repeating; I didn't learn how to write or get better at it until I started to write regularly and had made mistake after mistake after mistake. I developed a thick skin in order to improve. How would you react to your wife's criticism—always meant to help—every time you had her proofread one of your letters, stories or poems? "Don't you think a comma should go here?" "What exactly are you trying to say?" Truthfully, at times it was downright annoying, but I wanted the letter or the stories to be perfect so I just swallowed my pride and made the suggested changes. Then I read James Mitchner's autobiography, *The World is My Home, A Memoir*, and I learned how one of the best-selling authors of all time relied heavily on his editor—and not one editor, but many! He had an editor for content, one who checked the accuracy of his historical references, and another editor who looked for grammatical mistakes.

Ayn Rand wrote two best-selling novels: *Atlas Shrugged* and *The Fountainhead*. To fully appreciate how important editing and rewriting are to crafting a story—even for the most commercially successful writers—do yourself a favor and buy a copy of the Centennial Edition of her book *Anthem*. The last 158 pages of this edition contain a prior published edition of *Anthem* and include Rand's most recent handwritten corrections. If Ayn Rand had to go back and re-edit, then you and I should not feel bad about having to correct our mistakes.

If you are still not convinced that even the best writers make frequent errors and need to edit and re-write their material, get a copy of Bill Bryson's book *Shakespeare*. Speaking of the "greatest writer of all time," Mr. Bryson points out that Shakespeare:

> ...was routinely guilty of anatopisms—that is, getting one's geography wrong—particularly with regard to Italy, where so many of his plays were set. So in *The Taming of the Shrew* he puts a sailmaker in Bergamo, approximately the most landlocked city in the whole of Italy, while in *The Tempest* and *The Two Gentlemen of Verona* he has Prospero and Valentine set sail from, respectively, Milan and Verona, even though both cities were a good two days' travel from salt water. If he knew Venice had canals, he

gave no hint of it in either of the plays he set there. Whatever his other virtues, Shakespeare was not conspicuously worldly.

Anachronisms likewise abound in his plays. He has ancient Egyptians playing billiards and introduces the clock to Caesar's Rome fourteen hundred years before the first mechanical tick was heard there...[35]

If you have never seriously tried to write, you might ask if you should sign up for a writing class or a writer's seminar. I think the famous author, Stephen King, answers that question best in his book *On Writing*:

> You don't *need* writing classes or seminars any more than you need this or any other book on writing. Faulkner learned his trade while working in the Oxford, Mississippi, post office. Other writers have learned the basics while serving in the Navy, working in steel mills, or doing time in America's finer crossbar hotels. I learned the most valuable (and commercial) part of my life's work while washing motel sheets and restaurant tablecloths at the New Franklin Laundry in Bangor. You learn best by reading a lot and writing a lot, and the most valuable lessons of all are the ones you teach yourself....[36]

How does one go from being a non-writer to being an author? By writing! To write well requires a curious mind and a willingness to work hard, and it also requires you to be prepared to re-write and re-edit until the words speak the truth of your thoughts and experiences. It also helps to have an extensive vocabulary. Failure is an obligatory bump in your road. Expect it, and don't be afraid of it. Work through sloppy writing; tear up poorly written material and start again. Sometimes it won't be your writing that is bad or confusing; it will be your thinking. Learn to tell the difference.

Begin writing today. Write a letter to a friend or an e-mail to a relative. Start with a sentence, then move on to a paragraph. Avoid the common, parochial, and prosaic. Search out those life experiences that have had a major impact on you. Think about them carefully and then write about them in a fresh, original way. It will be fun and rewarding.

Writing is hard work. It takes discipline. I find that I do my best writing early in the morning before the world wakes up and distracts me. Do you realize that if you wrote only two pages a day, you could author a book of over seven hundred pages in one year? Most people don't even *read* seven hundred pages in a year!

Make sure before you start to write you have something to say that needs to be written down so it won't be lost. Everybody has these experiences. Don't forget my missionary experience. If you have nothing important to write about, nothing you do technically with the text will save it. If you only have diary entries of the inanities of your life, take it from me, your time will be better spent doing anything else.

Why did I write the Marciano Guzman story? At that time I didn't understand why I had to put the experience down on paper. Looking back—with the benefit of hindsight and maturity—I now understand a little better what was going on when I was inspired to sit and write what had happened that day in my office on Oasis Street in Indio, California.

Let me explain. I was not required to write the story or tell anyone about what had happened, but before the story could be written I had to fully understand it myself. That is the magic of writing; one cannot write clearly about what is not fully understood. And writing helps us to understand what we have lived. Although I didn't understand it at the time, my decision to write the story forced me to carefully consider what had happened and compelled me to sort out my reaction to the event before the actual writing could take place. Had I not made the decision to write the story I would not have gone through the exercise of thinking about what had happened. Events that are written give birth to thoughts that change behavior and shape the soul.

Hassan Bubacar Jallow

CHAPTER 4

HASSAN BUBACAR JALLOW

My life is my message: become an autodidact.

Become successful: take personal responsibility for your own education by expanding your vocabulary, reading voraciously, and learning to write. As of 2016, I have shared my message and this book with over 23,000 high school and college students all over the United States and Tanzania.

I am keenly aware of the fact that I am a child of privilege. My father was a doctor and my mother was a college graduate (UCLA). Nevertheless, it is important for the reader to understand that becoming an autodidact is a personal choice, and can be made by anyone; even someone from the humblest of circumstances and the poorest of countries.

I never met Abraham Lincoln, Nelson Mandela, or Winston Churchill. Like Frederick Douglass and the other autodidacts referenced in this book, I only know them secondhand from what they wrote and what was written about them. I know their stories, but not them.

But I do know Hassan Jallow. Mr. Jallow is the quintessential autodidact. Getting to know him and hearing his story makes my case that no matter where one is from, and no matter the obstacles one faces, success is within the reach of every motivated person.

What follows are excerpts from an interview I did with Hassan Jallow in my law office in Palm Desert, California, on April 19, 2009. At that time Mr. Jallow was in the United States giving speeches explaining the genocide case he was prosecuting for the United Nations in Arusha, Tanzania, against the former government leaders of Rwanda.

First a brief biographical sketch of Hassan Bubacar Jallow.

Hassan Bubacar Jallow of The Gambia was born in 1951 and studied law at the University of Dar Es Salaam, Tanzania, the Nigerian Law School, and at University College, London. He worked as State Attorney in the Attorney Generals' Chambers in The Gambia from 1976 until 1982 when he was appointed Solicitor General. Justice Hassan Bubacar Jallow served as The Gambia's Attorney General and Minister of Justice from 1984-2002. In 1998, he was appointed by the United Nations Secretary General to serve as an international legal expert and carry out a judicial evaluation of the International Criminal Tribunal for Rwanda and the International Criminal Tribunal for Yugoslavia. He also served as a legal expert for the Organization of African Unity and worked on the drafting and conclusion of the African Charter on Human and People's Rights, which was adopted in 1981. He has also served the Commonwealth in various respects including chairing the Governmental Working Group of Experts in Human Rights. Until his appointment as Prosecutor to the ICTR, Justice Jallow was a Judge of the Appeals Chamber of the Special Court for Sierra Leone on the appointment of the UN Secretary-General in 2002 as well as a member of the Commonwealth Secretariat Arbitral Tribunal. Justice Jallow was awarded the honor of Commander of the National Order of the Republic of Gambia.

P: To understand the significance of the cases you are prosecuting, why don't you give us some background as to what happened in Rwanda and how that relates to what you are doing in Tanzania today.

J: Rwanda is next door to Tanzania; they share a border. Rwanda is a small country comprised, basically, of three ethnic groups: Tutsi, Hutu, and Twa. The majority of the population is Hutu. In 1994 there was a genocide in Rwanda which lasted one hundred days, from April sixth up until July. In the course of those one hundred days, over one million Tutsis were killed by extremist groups and by members of the armed forces and the government...After that, the United Nations set up a tribunal to prosecute those persons responsible for these offenses, and basically the offenses were genocide, crimes against humanity, and war crimes.

Under the statute of the tribunal, there is an office of Chief Prosecutor. This person is responsible for organizing the investigations and the prosecutions of those people who were responsible for the genocide. So that is the job I am doing there now.

We have a staff of close to a thousand at the moment, and they are drawn from ninety countries, which is in line with the principles of the United Nations. We recruit internationally; people representing ninety countries, all the major legal traditions, all the different cultures and religions of the world. So there is a lot of diversity at the tribunal.

P: Based on your investigations and your trials, how were most of the people killed during that one hundred day period?

J: The genocide was different from a war, and there was a war going on in Rwanda at the time. There was a rebel army. They had organized and were fighting the government, to overthrow it, because the government was an extremist, undemocratic government which had no respect for human rights. So, there was that conflict going on, and in the course of that conflict, the government turned on its own people, the minority Tutsis, with a view toward exterminating them.

The nature of that genocide was different from the armed conflict because the genocide was really carried out by ordinary people and by the military and by the militia. Most of the killing was done by cutlass or machete and so all of the activity was done at very close quarters. You had to be very close to the person you were killing. You find that, most of the time, it was a situation of people who knew each other turning against each other and killing each other. Neighbors turned against each other. The people you have been living next door to for ages suddenly became your enemy and you wiped them out. Doctors turned upon patients they had been attending to in hospitals. In churches, you had clergy betraying the flock which they had been ministering to every Sunday. It was something very close and very personal. You even had family members turning on each other because they were from different ethnic groups; husband against wife, and so on. It was a very personal, close thing.

P: Can you give us some idea of the basic problem between the Hutus and the Tutsis that caused this outrageous, inhumane attack?

J: Earlier I described them as two ethnic groups: Tutsis and Hutus. The Hutus were the vast majority; the Tutsis constituted less than 20 percent of the population at the time. But they speak the same language, so essentially they are almost one and the same ethnic group, but they have different physical features. Historically, the Tutsis had been the actual rulers of Rwanda. They provided the monarchy. They ran the feudal system, which governed Rwanda. But when colonialism came, with the Belgians and the Germans, the Europeans more or less institutionalized that arrangement into one of racial superiority and racial inferiority. They developed all kinds of theories and hypotheses that the Tutsis were actually different, that they had come from a different place and that they were superior—racially superior. As a result, you had feelings of superiority being developed amongst the Tutsi and feelings of inferiority and anger and oppression being developed among the Hutus. Then came 1959 when independence was granted to Rwanda. There were elections and a government came into being that was based on majority rule. And this meant, essentially, that the Hutu government was placed in power. Unfortunately, this government was comprised mainly of extremists and gradually you found these extremists, now in positions of authority in the government and in the military, sanctioning mass killing of the Tutsis—but nothing on the scale of what was to occur in 1994.

The ground for 1994 had also been well prepared in a number of other ways by the Hutu extremists who were in power. There was always a lot of propaganda through the radio, through writings, newspapers, etc., describing the Tutsi minority as the cause of all the problems that Rwanda faced. This is reminiscent of how Hitler dealt with the Jewish people. The Nazis blamed the Jews for everything that went wrong. And the same thing in Rwanda; they blamed the Tutsi minority for everything that was going on.

In the fight that they were having with the rebels, the military officially described the enemy to include Tutsi civilians. This actually qualifies as a war crime because these were innocent civilians who had nothing to do with the war. That is the background.

On April 6, 1994, the plane carrying the president of Rwanda was shot down and the extremists used this as an excuse to turn on the minority. They blamed them for the loss of the president, for the death of the president. However, there is evidence that suggests that it was actually the extremists who planned and executed the assassination because there had been negotiations between the president and the Tutsis for a settlement, for a peace settlement. And that peace settlement would have brought the Tutsis into the government.

And so the belief is that the extremists didn't want that, so they turned on their own president, killed him and then blamed the minority for what had happened. And that let loose the genocide.

P: For those who read this interview, who don't understand the ethnicity in Rwanda, Hutus and Tutsis are both black. Is this correct?

J: They are both black, yes.

P: What you are doing in Tanzania with this court is argu-
ably the most important criminal prosecution on earth
at the present time, and I wanted to hold this interview
so that everybody could understand how important
your position is. But I have also been to your home
town in The Gambia, which is a very little village named
Bansang. You said that they only have electricity seven
hours a day.

J: Yes.

P: And I want to ask you how it is possible that Hassan Jallow, born in The Gambia, which is the poorest country
in Africa, ended up by becoming the most important
prosecutor in the world in the year 2009? I would like
to have you back up and tell us about your childhood
in The Gambia and how you ended up doing what you
have done with your life.

J: I was born in Bansang, which is a little village about
315 kilometers away from the city. Bansang sits on the
banks of the River Gambia. I was born in 1951.

I thank God and my parents that I have come a long
way from Bansang up to this position as the Chief Prosecutor. I am an Under Secretary General of the United
Nations as well. The journey was long and it was not
always easy. I was fortunate to have parents who were
very keen to see us go through school. My father was
a religious leader, an Imam. He didn't have any formal
education, even in the Arabic language, but he was a
person who was always devoted to reading and writing.
He wrote a great deal, and he preached. My mother was

a kind woman who was very dedicated to ensuring that we went through school and that we succeeded.

P: Back when you were born, what percentage of the population of The Gambia was literate and could read and write?

J: Must have less than two digits at that time. Below 10 percent I'm sure.

P: And your family—up until the time your brother went to high school, how many members of your family had graduated from high school?

J: We were the first generation in the family to go to school. Nobody else had. My elder brother was the first to go into high school and then I followed suit with the other brothers. Our generation was the first generation of the family to go to school.

P: What is the rate of literacy in The Gambia today?

J: It is slightly higher now. It is probably closer to 20, 30 percent.

P: And what is the average life expectancy for a man or woman in The Gambia today?

J: Just below fifty now.

P: And the average wage?

J: In U.S. dollar terms it would be approximately $40 to $50 per month.

P: Let's go back to your childhood. You had no role model of anybody having gone to college. You had no lawyers in the family. What is your first memory of learning anything?

J: My first memory is of my father. He was very busy, always reading and writing and teaching the Qur'an and religion. That's my first memory of reading and writing. And, of course, he took us through that sort of religious instruction as well.

P: You are a Muslim?

J: I am Muslim. My father took us through reading and writing of the Qur'an.

I think largely I developed my love for reading and writing because of him, because this was something he was constantly engaged in. There was a primary school in the village but we didn't go to school early. We went a little bit late. There were only two high schools in The Gambia at that time, in the whole country. There was a high school close in a town some ten miles from my village, which had been established specifically as a school for the sons of chiefs in the country. Then you had another school, which was run by the Methodist Mission. It is now called The Gambia High School. But I had developed a love of reading from my father and I recall that even before I enrolled there, I would go to the little primary school; I would stand by the window, outside on the veranda, watching, looking into the classroom. I had a little scrap of paper with me on the veranda and I would be trying to write what they were doing inside the class because we had not yet been sent to school. I thought one of the teachers would drive me away the first time he saw me but, when he noticed me there, he encouraged me to stay on. And he also came to see my father about getting us into school. His name was Mr. Hassan Njie.

From an early age, I had developed an interest in reading, and an old man sent us six boys to school. My elder brother was the first to go to high school. He was about four years older than myself. He went to high school, and I followed suit, but before I went into high school, I read my brother's books, the books he had been using in high school. My first day of high school, when we got our supply of books, I opened one of them. It was a French book and the teacher looked at me and said, "Where did you learn to read this? This is just your first day in Form 1 in high school."

I said, "I used to read my brother's books, my elder brother's books." So I had an appetite for reading.

In high school I was also a member of the National Library. I was a member of the junior section, but when I read all the junior section holdings the chief librarian promoted me to the senior section. And it was not easy reading because, as I said, when I was a child in primary school, there was no electricity in the village. At least now there are seven hours a day. We used candlelight to read. We used a hurricane lamp with gasoline to read. We read by firelight. And even when I got into high school, in the city, most of the time we would not have electricity in the house so we would have to take our books outside and sit under the streetlights at night. We'd go there after school and that's where we read.

Sometimes we would go to the post office because the post office was always well lit. You would find groups of us sitting on the veranda of the post office, where the lights were, reading our books up to midnight. Then we'd go back home.

P: Why was reading so important to you?

J: It was important, not so much because of any career thoughts as such but, even at that early age, I discovered that reading really took me very much beyond my village, very much beyond my country. It opened the world to me.

Through a book, you could see the rest of the world. You could understand the rest of the world. You learned about new things that you couldn't see, and that was very, very fascinating. The book represented this kind of thing—of learning so much beyond your own immediate area. And so, as a child, I tried to read everything I could find, whether at home or in the library. I remember even when I used to go back to the village on holidays from the city I always made a point of going to the National Library and picking up a dozen books. If I went home for Christmas holidays I would pick up a dozen books. I put them in a carton and I went with them. And I had a very sympathetic and understanding chief librarian. She was a very nice and very kind person. She allowed me to take as many books as I wanted—but I always brought them back intact. The book really was a door which opened the rest of the world to me, even at that early age. I learned so much.

P: When did you first realize that you needed to have a large vocabulary in order to enjoy life and be successful?

J: I think it was during the transition from primary school to high school. In order to do this, you had to take an exam. I did that at an early age, but the exam was essentially English and math, and I wasn't good at mathematics. On the day the results came out, I was sitting in the school. I was feeling disappointed because I hadn't had any news of the results, whether I had gone through or not. And then Father Flynn of the Roman Catholic mission, a teacher at the high school, came into the town and he sent for me. He said, "Your math isn't very good but your English is outstanding, and that's why you are going on to high school." Right then I knew that language was very, very important. Language was getting me into high school. And gradually, over the years, the system of education that we had in the Catholic school helped me develop my vocabulary and my writing skills.

My school had a practice of calling everybody back to school on Saturday morning at 9:00. Everybody came back to school to write an essay on a topic that had been selected by the teacher. And we did that for six years. Every Saturday, except holidays, you came back to high school, and you sat down and you wrote an essay for one hour. This all helped me to develop the vocabulary and develop the language skills that I found so useful as a lawyer because, as a lawyer, you are dealing with language skills. You are dealing with ideas.

P: Where do you think you would be today if you had never learned how to read?

J: I don't know where I would be, but I think I would have probably been less fortunate. I would have missed out on so much in the world. In its few pages, a book enables you to discover things which are out of your immediate vicinity, which are far removed in time and space from where you are, but you are able to learn about them and to understand them. I would have missed a lot of this.

P: Your father was an Imam in the Muslim faith. What does the Qur'an say about the individual's responsibility for learning to read, write, speak, think?

J: The Qur'an and the Holy Prophet Muhammad place a lot of emphasis on knowledge. You will find many instances in the Holy Qur'an where it talks about the signs of the existence of God, and it describes in many places the kind of people to whom these signs are visible. And it starts off by saying that these signs are visible to men of knowledge. Then it talks of them being visible to men of faith, to men of understanding, and so on. Therefore, knowledge is one of the prerequisites for being able to understand the signs of the existence of God as found in the Qur'an. Also, the Holy Prophet Muhammad, peace be upon him, emphasized the obligation of every Muslim to go and search for and acquire knowledge. One of his famous sayings is that if you have to go all the way to China to acquire a piece of knowledge, you should do so. In other words, no matter what the distance, how far away information is, you have a duty to go and find it where it is and get it. So knowledge is a prerequisite under Islam for good faith. It is an obligation also, put upon every person, to try to reach out and acquire it.

P: Tell me about books you have enjoyed, that have had a great impact on your life.

J: This is difficult, but some of the books that stand out include Shakespeare's plays, because William Shakespeare says so many things that are so wise and yet so evident. They may seem obvious, but you don't always get to hear about them. They stick with you. He is one of the authors I have always enjoyed. We read a lot of his plays in high school: *Julius Caesar, Romeo and Juliet,*

King Lear, and all the rest of them.

On the spiritual side, I have been guided by books written by my father, of course, and also by Muhammad Ghazali. He was born in Iraq and is a great Islamic philosopher and Sufi who has written very, very extensively. He has been another important influence on me as well.

P: I have read one of your father's books and was very impressed by it. It seems that all great religions emphasize knowledge and individual responsibility, whether that individual is a Mormon, a Jew, a Muslim—whatever they might be. Why do you think that, today, young people might not have the same desire to seek learning through books that you had growing up in Bansang?

J: I think these days that, perhaps, the educational system is not as rigorous as it used to be, as disciplined as it used to be. When we were in school, in our time, you had English and math and reading and writing. It was tough. You had to study hard. These days it is a little bit more liberal and almost wishy-washy, shall I say. Then there are the distractions. This generation has too many distractions. I mean, television, electronic games, telephones, et cetera.

So we really have to keep our children away from a lot of these distractions and try to get them to focus on the important things: reading, communicating, going out and doing physical play, and physical work. There is less and less of that, and I think the children lose because of this.

P: What role does a parent have in making sure that children read?

J: The parent has an important role. I think you don't even, as a parent, always have to tell the child to go and read. Just let the child see you pick up a book and sit down and read. If the child looks around and sees both parents are reading every evening, he will probably pick up a book without being told to do so. You teach by example. And as I said earlier, you guide them away from a lot of distractions into some of these more productive activities.

P: Do you enjoy biographies and history?

J: History. I have read a lot of history.

P: What do you take away from the history books that you read?

J: Well, that the world changes. There are many changes, though there is also much that remains constant. History, as they always say, is extremely important for an understanding of the present. If you want to understand what's going on now, you need to go back into history. Most of the situations in which we find ourselves have an historical explanation and so knowing history is very important. But these days I find I read more religion and religious philosophy than anything else, that is, when it comes to anything outside of my own specialization.

P: I have explained to you the reason why I am writing this book. I want to get this information out to high school students and college students. I want to encourage the study of vocabulary, reading, and writing. If you were in front of a group of American high school students who have their electricity 24/7, who have libraries that have more books than they could ever read in a lifetime—based on your life, what would you tell them about the importance of reading?

J: If you want to be able to sit down in one place and know something about the rest of the world and about man's history and understand the present, you have to simply open up a book and read. It is the easiest way to obtain knowledge about all those matters. A book is a gateway to knowing and understanding the world. And, as a human being, you are obliged to try and know and understand the world. A book also enables you to travel while remaining in one place. You travel over space and you travel over time just by opening and turning pages and reading them. The book also helps you to be a better communicator, and communication is so important.

P: How about the journey into your soul? Is it possible to get into your own soul without reading?

J: Well, you could do this, I imagine, without reading, but you would need to be quite open to yourself and be quite frank with yourself and to be very introspective as well, I suppose. But being able to read and reading the spiritual philosophy books would help significantly.

P: What are you looking for when you read spiritual books now? You are already a devout Muslim. You say your prayers. You have done the Hajj. You do all the things that a devout Muslim does, so why do you need to read anything? What is it that you are reaching for?

J: When I read or when I practice religion, I want to be closer to God. That is the objective—to be closer to God. And there are many ways you can do this. You can go beyond just doing the obligatory rituals.

You can read books that help you in improving your own contact with God and that try to make you a better person. There are books which will open doors to you through which you can walk onto a path to God, for example, those of Ghazali in which he explains a number of practices, Sufi practices of meditation and of worship, that you can undertake.

P: There are so many different paths you can take with your life. For example, even being born into a wealthy family you can lead a very hedonistic, self-indulgent life and then die. How does reading, building your vocabulary, and writing help a person avoid the pitfalls of the carnal, the sensual, and go on to become a productive member of society. How do those disciplines help you avoid the pitfalls?

J: If you are an avid reader, and you are an understanding reader, you read so that you can learn. You learn from the experiences of others. You learn how things can go wrong and have gone wrong with others in the past. You learn from all of that, and this learning can help you along the right path. So, in other words, you read with a view to drawing lessons which can help you avoid some of these pitfalls. I think reading can be useful in that sense.

P: Why did you choose to live a life of public service as opposed to choosing to make a fortune for yourself? Why did you choose public service?

J: First, because my father insisted that I do this, and secondly because I liked it. When I told him I was going to read law, he wasn't very happy about it because there is this perception that lawyers—you know, that they just want the money. He said to me, "Well, okay. You can go read law but I think it is best if you devote your service to the public, to the community, rather than being a private lawyer." And I agreed with him. I said, "That is what I will do." For my whole career, apart from two or three years, I have been in public service. I did spend two years as a private practitioner, but this was against my will. I had been in the government as attorney general and the military came in and overthrew the government, so my appointment ended. I went into private practice in order to keep body and soul together, but my heart wasn't in it and I was happy to go back into the Supreme Court as a justice. All of my brothers, as well, are public servants. None of them has worked in the private sector.

P: I went to a prison in Utah because I was interested in finding out what they had in common, other than the fact that they were criminals. And I found out they were all illiterate. They couldn't read. I asked the warden about this and he said that, actually, about 55 percent of the prisoners are illiterate. Then I talked with my brother-in-law, who is in the prison system as a psychologist, and he said that illiteracy is a serious problem among criminals.

I know you are dealing with a completely different group of malefactors in the tribunals, but is it your experience as the Attorney General and then as an official in The Gambia that most of the prisoners—the people who turn to crime—can't read or write?

J: That is true. Ignorance is a major factor in criminology, even in Rwanda; whereas the kind of criminals we are prosecuting—the top leadership—are literate, educated people. The fact is that the genocide occurred because these people were able to convince the ignorant, ordinary people on the street that this was the right thing to do. These illiterate people just swallowed the propaganda that was being fed to them by the literate people and carried out this monstrous offense. So you have a situation where, if you had had people who were sufficiently well-educated to understand that all people have rights—well, it would have been very difficult, if not impossible, to get them to carry out this genocide. I think ignorance is a major contributor to crime.

P: When you were growing up, did anybody make fun of you for studying, for reading in any light you could find? Did they think you were crazy?

J: Well, they teased me sometimes. They called me bookworm. Some would call me that, but there were others doing what I was doing. And I had friends who had the same interests, so we were together. These friends have also gone very far in life, thank God.

P: Tell me about your family. Where are your children?

J: I have five children—four boys and a girl. The youngest one is fourteen; she is the girl. Two of the kids have just graduated university. One is studying law; the other is in environmental science. One other is in Canada and the other is in the U.K. The girl is with us in Arusha. My wife is Gambian also, and she was a senior civil servant.

P: Do you read the Qur'an every day?

J: Every day. As a Muslim, if you do your prayers, this means that every day you have to read the Qur'an. You have to recite portions of the Qur'an from memory in every prayer.

P: So you read the Qur'an every day and then you read in your work every day and then you read for personal enrichment and enjoyment. How many hours a day do you think you read?

J: Outside of the official reading, maybe an hour a day. That's reading away from the office.

P: And at work?

J: In the office, you read. You are in meetings. Basically that is what you do. That's it. And you do research. Although I have a large staff that helps me with much of this, I still have to read it when it is done.

P: If you were in charge of The Gambia—or all of Africa— what would be your number one priority?

J: My number one priority would be education. I think education is the key to development in Africa. We need to have compulsory education at all levels, and you need to have this education available and accessible to everybody at all levels in Africa. When people go to school, when they go to university, they acquire skills. They become professionals. They can take care of themselves and they can take care of their families. They know how to take care of their health problems. Education is the best way of lifting the standards of progress in the community. I think we spend a lot of resources now on helping the poor, on trying to build infrastructure, on trying to develop health facilities, and so on and so forth. But the best way we can do this is to help people to be able to help themselves and that you do through getting them to acquire education and skills.

P: Can you have education in Africa if the population remains illiterate?

J: No. If I had billions of dollars at my disposal, I would put that money into schools. I would make sure, of course, that there were schools at all levels and that they were available to everybody and then I would make sure it was compulsory for everybody to attend them. You have to do that, and if you do do that over a generation you will see a tremendous change in the society.

P: I have good friends who are Muslims and I know that as a Muslim you are disciplined to pray five times a day. You are disciplined to memorize certain verses of the Qur'an. You are disciplined to read the Qur'an. What role do you believe discipline has played in your success?

J: Well, again, I think my father and my mother were very influential. They helped to bring a sense of objective, purpose, and order into my life. I also was helped by an uncle with whom I lived while I was in high school in the city.

One has to discipline oneself for one's own sake, for the sake of one's soul and for one's future. You can't make progress without learning to control your desires, controlling yourself, trying to identify what is right and what is wrong and focusing on what is essential. If you don't do that you will almost be like a leaf in the wind.

I think self-discipline is absolutely vital and I have been fortunate to have parents and relatives who helped me with that.

P: Hassan, I want you to put yourself in the place of someone who did not have this good home life, whose parents divorced and whose mother, maybe, is a drug addict or an alcoholic and this young person is in high school. How do you communicate to this person the importance of discipline? How do you teach it to him?

J: Actually, you can overcome these disadvantages, if you discipline yourself. In my office there is a young man who is a "Tri-Latin", who grew up as a child soldier. He was captured when he was barely ten and conscripted into an army of rebels and at that young age he did tremendous things, using guns and so on. Today he is a trial attorney in my office. He lifted himself above what had happened to him; he made sure he went to high school. He then went on to university and to law school. He read. Now he's involved in prosecuting people who do those horrible things—abducting children and conscripting them into rebel armies and making them commit war crimes and crimes against humanity. And he can help because he overcame these obstacles.

Even when you come from a poor background, you have the ability to overcome it. And I think reading, dedicating yourself to study, is one of the ways you do it. That's what this young man did. He escaped from the rebels, made sure he got enrolled in school, and before he knew it, he was in a university in Canada reading law.

P: When you say, "He was conscripted into the rebel army," you are talking about a ten-year old boy being given orders to kill other people.

J: Yes.

P: Face to face, with guns, knives, everything.

J;   He did that.

P: And he went from that life into the one he has now, where he is a prosecutor, and the way he did this was by disciplining himself, by reading?

J: By disciplining himself. By committing himself to reading and educating himself—he used the opportunities that came to him and so he moved out of that life into something much better.

P: Do you think Allah—your Allah/our God, it's one in the same—puts in the heart of every person the ability to do this if they choose to do it, regardless of their circumstances?

J: Yes. I think that God gives us enormous opportunities and it is up to us to seize them.

P: The name of my book is *Autodidactic: Self-Taught,* and I look at it this way: You can have good teachers or bad teachers, good parents or bad parents, good friends or bad friends, but when everybody goes to bed at night, the only person that each of us has in our head is ourselves. And so knowing that Allah/God put in me the ability to turn myself around—if I want to—puts the responsibility squarely on my shoulders and not on my teachers, not on my priest, not on my Imam, and not on my parents. And so I think we have a universal understanding of that. But the point is: how do we get our young people to understand this?

J: I think we have to talk to them more. For instance the young person I told you about, who was a child soldier and is now a prosecutor, is planning to go around to some of these conflict areas in order to speak to children who are in a similar situation or who have just come out of a similar situation, to help them understand that with discipline and commitment they can become like him or become even better than he is. We need to communicate this to these children.

P: Recently a poll was taken among many of the great historians and they were asked what they considered to be the most important event in terms of the development of civilization. All of these historians pointed to the Gutenberg printing press because, they said, once we got the printing press it became possible for ordinary people to read religious texts and other works. The invention of the printing press was the seminal moment in the history of mankind. And now with the Internet and the ability we have to research and read—well, it's amazing. You have the whole world open to you. You can access it. You can read about it.

J: When I'm traveling, my little girl in Arusha will tell me, "When you get to New York, can you go to such and such a street? There is a shop there and I want you to buy me this." I say, "How do you know about this? You've never been there." She says, "Don't worry. I checked it on the Internet."

P: Because she can read.

J: Because she can read and she can go to the Internet and find out what she wants to know and then tell me, who goes to New York all the time but doesn't know where those places are.

P: I can remember the first time I was in the Serengeti. I'm in the middle of the forest watching the animals and I see a Maasai woman herding cattle. And I was all set to take her picture—my finger was already on the button. All of a sudden she pulls out a cell phone! This is in the middle of the Serengeti! I could have been in the middle of New York!

J: It's true.

P: You and I may come from different cultures, we may

belong to different religions, but we have in common the fact that we read the same books. We think the same thoughts, and we think in terms of trying to help other people.

In 2006, at the invitation of Hassan Jallow, I traveled to The Gambia to meet with the president and other leaders of the country. I was there to explore the possibility of facilitating several humanitarian projects. Hassan Jallow was going to be my host. Unfortunately, when I arrived in the capital city of Banjul, I was told that Mr. Jallow would not be seeing me this trip; his brother had died, and he was in mourning with the family in their home village of Bansang, hundreds of miles from the capital.

After meeting with President Yahya Jammeh and several other government officials, I made arrangements to be taken by car to Bansang to see my good friend Hassan, and to pay my respects to the family. After two harrowing crossings of the Gambia River in an unseaworthy, overcrowded ferry (there are no bridges over the Gambia River, even though the river bisects the entire country), and eight hours in a Toyota Land Cruiser being driven too fast over partially paved roads, I finally arrived in Bansang.

Bansang is exactly what an experienced world traveler would expect of a small village in the poorest country in Africa. The smell of poverty, open sewers and burning garbage is unmistakable and overwhelming. Nevertheless, the people are welcoming and friendly.

Even in 2006, Hassan Jallow's father's house—where Hassan was raised—has no front door; only a blanket covering the entrance. There are openings for windows, but no glass. The floor is hard-packed dirt. There is electricity, but not 24 hours a day. Meals are cooked outside on a bed of charcoal. Sitting on the veranda of the Jallow house, I could not help but marvel at the extraordinary journey Hassan had made from his home village of Bansang to the Security Council of the United Nations.

I am sure that many of the students I speak to here in the United States have difficult lives and face daunting challenges. Nevertheless, I hope that by reading Hassan Jallow's interview, the young people of the world will gain perspective, and truly understand that there is hope. Success in life is personal. Hassan Jallow is proof that anyone, from anywhere, can become successful—no matter where they are from, and no matter how difficult their circumstances.

The key to success is found deep within the individual. Parents help, teachers help, peers help. But at the end of the day, unless one takes personal responsibility for one's own education and becomes an autodidact, one will encounter one insuperable problem after another.

"Insuperable?"

Look it up!

CHAPTER 5

THE LAST WORD

My life and *my* experiences have proven to me that the key to *your* future is based on *your* vocabulary, *your* exposure to literature and *your* ability to write. This is true regardless of your career path.

I hear what you are saying: "Mr. Parkinson, you don't know me. My father left my mother, and my brother is a drug dealer." "I am too far behind to catch up." "My teachers think I am stupid." "I don't have a quiet place where I can read." "I don't have money to buy books." "Furthermore, your examples and quotes from Winston Churchill do not apply to me. I come from a really poor family."

Get serious—Go tell that to Frederick Douglass, Malcolm X, or Hassan Jallow.

Abraham Lincoln did not have a formal education. He did not have a computer, an iPod or Internet access. As a matter of fact he did not have access to an indoor toilet or hot running water for most of his life. A lot of people said he was ugly, awkward, and that he didn't have a clue how to dress himself appropriately. How did this boy from the backwoods of Kentucky ever become the President of the United States of America? How did a "rail-splitting, country lawyer"—who did not attend an Ivy-League law school, or any law school for that matter—save the Union and also author and deliver the two most famous speeches ever given on American soil—his Second Inaugural Address and the Gettysburg Address?

How did he do it? Like Winston Churchill, Frederick Douglass, Malcolm X, Hassan Jallow, and many others, Abraham Lincoln was an autodidact.

Still unsure how to succeed? You can read about the Romans or you can ask Hassan Jallow. The principles of success are the same today as they were two thousand years ago. Don't delude yourself into thinking that other people are "gifted," and therefore that is why they are successful. That is the lazy man's reasoning. They understood the game and they paid the price to become great. Are you willing to do the same? Go out and buy a pocket dictionary and carry it with you. Look up words. Stop numbing your mind with television, spectator sports, and games. Start to read, develop a healthy curiosity, and begin a meaningful journal. Remember:

> The credit belongs to the man who is actually in the arena, whose face is marred by dust and sweat and blood, who knows the great enthusiasms, the great devotions, and spends himself in a worthy cause; who at best, if he wins, knows the thrills of high achievements, and, if he fails, at least fails daring greatly, so that his place shall never be with those cold and timid souls who know neither victory nor defeat.
>
> *Theodore Roosevelt*

AFTERWORD

My daughter, Brooke Parkinson, was extremely helpful in editing and making suggestions for this book. When Brooke completed her last reading of the book she asked me where my list was for books I recommended. I told her I didn't think anybody would want to have a list from me. Brooke disagreed. She convinced me that at least one person—Brooke—wanted the list. What follows is not an exhaustive list, but simply books that I have read that I think most people would enjoy and find informative.

AUTOBIOGRAPHIES

The Autobiography of Benjamin Franklin

The Autobiography of Malcolm X as told to Alex Haley

My Life So Far, by Jane Fonda

Long Walk to Freedom: The Autobiography of Nelson Mandela

Narrative of the Life of Frederick Douglass, An American Slave and *Incidents in the Life of a Slave Girl*

Promises to Keep: On Life and Politics, by Joe Biden

The World Is My Home, by James A. Michener

The Autobiography of Eleanor Roosevelt

Autobiography: The Story of My Experiments with Truth, by M.K. Gandhi

Open, by Andre Agassi

BIOGRAPHIES

Eisenhower: Soldier and President, by Stephen E. Ambrose

Lindbergh, by A. Scott Berg

Joseph Smith: Rough Stone Rolling, by Richard Lyman Bushman

Master of the Senate: The Years of Lyndon Johnson, by Robert A. Caro

Path to Power (The Years of Lyndon Johnson, Volume 1), by Robert A. Caro

Means of Ascent (The Years of Lyndon Johnson, Volume 2), by Robert A. Caro

Titan: The Life of John D. Rockefeller, Sr., by Ron Chernow

No Ordinary Time: Franklin and Eleanor Roosevelt: The Home Front in WWII, by Doris Kearns Goodwin

Lyndon Johnson and the American Dream, by Doris Kearns Goodwin

Go Forward with Faith: The Biography of Gordon B. Hinckley, by Sheri L. Dew

A Godly Hero: The Life of William Jennings Bryan, by Michael Kazin

Lengthen Your Stride: The Presidency of Spencer W. Kimball, by Edward L. Kimball

John Adams, by David McCullough

Truman, by David McCullough

American Caesar: Douglas MacArthur 1880–1964, by William Manchester

The Last Lion: Winston Spencer Churchill: Visions of Glory, 1874-1932, by William Manchester

When Pride Still Mattered: A Life of Vince Lombardi, by David Maraniss

The Rise of Theodore Roosevelt, by Edmund Morris

The Chief: The Life of William Randolph Hurst, by David Nasaw

Justice For All: Earl Warren and the Nation He Made, by Jim Newton

King of the World: Muhammed Ali and the Rise of an American Hero, by David Remnick

FDR, by Jean Edward Smith

Grant, by Jean Edward Smith

John Marshall: Definer of a Nation, by Jean Edward Smith

The Man to See: Edward Bennett Williams: Ultimate Insider; Legendary Trial Lawyer, by Evan Thomas

Soul of the Lion: A Biography of General Joshua L. Chamberlain, by Willard M. Wallace

Sandy Koufax: A Lefty's Legacy, by Jane Leary

Alexander Hamilton, by Ron Chernow

Mornings on Horseback: The Story of an Extraordinary Family, a Vanished Way of Life and the Unique Child Who Became Theodore Roosevelt, by David McCullough

Wheels for the World, by Douglas Brinkley

Washington, by Ron Chernow

Killing Reagan, by Bill O'Reilly and Martin Dugan

RELIGION

The Bible

The Book of Mormon

Genesis, by Bill Moyers

The Koran

The Pagan Christ: Is Blind Faith Killing Christianity?, by Tom Harpur

Religious Literacy: What Every American Needs to Know—And Doesn't, by Stephen Prothero

Speaking of Faith: Why Religion Matters and How to Talk About It, by Krista Tippett

EDUCATIONAL

On Writing, by Stephen King

Eats, Shoots & Leaves : The Zero Tolerance Approach to Punctuation, by Lynne Truss

Pedagogy of the Oppressed, by Paulo Freire and Myra Bergman Ramos

Literacies of Power, by Donaldo Macedo

Make It Stick, by Brown, Roediger and McDaniel

Talent Is Overrated: What Really Separates World-Class Performers from Everybody Else, by Geoff Colvin

The Seven Sins of Memory, by Daniel Schacter

Mindset, by Carol Dwick

GENERAL FICTION

I Know Why the Caged Bird Sings, Maya Angelou

In Cold Blood, by Truman Capote

The Red Badge of Courage and Selected Short Fiction, by Stephen Crane

Deliverance, by James Dickey

A Time To Kill, by John Grisham

A Farewell to Arms, by Ernest Hemingway

For Whom the Bell Tolls, by Ernest Hemingway

The Gaucho Martin Fierro, by Jose Hernandez

Kite Runner, by Khaled Hosseini

The Air Between Us, by Deborah Johnson

To Kill a Mockingbird, by Harper Lee

Arrowsmith, by Sinclair Lewis

Elmer Gantry, by Sinclair Lewis

Main Street, by Sinclair Lewis

Lonesome Dove, by Larry McMurtry

Atlas Shrugged, by Ayn Rand

The Fountainhead, by Ayn Rand

All Quiet on the Western Front, by Erich Maria Remarque

The Lovely Bones, by Alice Sebold

East of Eden, by John Steinbeck

The Grapes of Wrath, by John Steinbeck

Uncle Tom's Cabin, by Harriet Beecher Stowe

Huckleberry Finn, by Mark Twain

The Onion Field, by Joseph Wambaugh

The Caine Mutiny, by Herman Wouk

War and Remembrance, by Herman Wouk

Winds of War, by Herman Wouk

Black Boy, by Richard Wright

Native Son, by Richard Wright

GENERAL NON-FICTION

Letter to My Daughter, by Maya Angelou

An Army at Dawn: The War in North Africa, 1942-1943, by Rick Atkinson

In Plain Sight: The Startling Truth Behind the Elizabeth Smart Investigation, by Tom Smart and Lee Benson

Flags of our Fathers, by James Bradley with Ron Powers

Palestine: Peace Not Apartheid, by Jimmy Carter

The Speed of Trust, by Stephen M. R. Covey

Faith and Politics: How the "Moral Values" Debate Divides America and How to Move Forward Together, by Senator John Danforth

The World Is Flat: A Brief History of the Twenty-First Century, by Thomas L. Friedman

In Search of Bill Clinton: A Psychological Biography, by John D. Gartner

Team of Rivals: The Political Genius of Abraham Lincoln, by Doris Kearns Goodwin

Wait Till Next Year, by Doris Kearns Goodwin

Left to Tell: Discovering God Amongst the Rwandan Holocaust, by Immaculee Ilibagiza

The Challenge for Africa, by Wangari Maathai

Gift from the Sea, by Anne Morrow Lindbergh

Goodbye, Darkness: A Memoir of the Pacific War, by William Manchester

The Fate of Africa: A History of Fifty Years of Independence, by Martin Meredith

The River of Doubt: Theodore Roosevelt's Darkest Journey, by Candice Millard

Moyers on Democracy, by Bill Moyers

Dead Aid: Why Aid Is Not Working and How There Is a Better Way for Africa, by Dambisa Moyo

Patriotic Grace: What It Is and Why We Need It Now, by Peggy Noonan

When Character Was King: A Story of Ronald Reagan, by Peggy Noonan

Soldier Slaves: Abandoned by the White House, Courts, and Congress, by James W. Parkinson and Lee Benson

Blood and Thunder: The Epic Story of Kit Carson and the Conquest of the American West, by Hampton Sides

Ghost Soldiers: The Forgotten Epic Story of World War II's Most Dramatic Mission, by Hampton Sides

Manhunt: The 12-Day Chase for Lincoln's Killer, by James L. Swanson

Sea of Thunder: Four Commanders and the Last Great Naval Campaign 1941-1945, by Evan Thomas

Blood Done Sign My Name, by Timothy B. Tyson

The War Lovers, by Evan Thomas

ENDNOTES

1. Eugene Cernan and Don Davis, *The Last Man on the Moon* (New York: St. Martin's Griffin, 1999), 208-209.

2. The Doctrine and Covenants is a book of revelations received by Mormon prophets, starting with Joseph Smith in the early 1800s.

3. Edward Gibbon, *The Decline and Fall of the Roman Empire* (New York: Random House, 2003), 16-17.

4. Geoff Colvin, *Talent Is Overrated: What* Really *Separates World-Class Performers from Everybody Else* (New York: Penguin Group, 2008), 6.

5. Ibid., 27.

6. Ibid., 30-31.

7. Ibid., 62.

8. The actual quotation is found in his book, *The World is Flat,* and reads as follows: "There comes a time when you've got to put away the Game Boys, turn off the television set, put away the iPod, and get your kids down to work."

9. I recently learned that "desirable difficulties" and "frequent testing" are proven pedagogical tools for effective learning (Bjork, R.A. (1994). Memory and metamemory

considerations in the training of human beings. In J. Metcalfe and A. Shimamura (Eds.), *Metacognition: Knowing about Knowing* (pp. 185-205). Cambridge, MA: MIT Press; *The Power of Testing Memory, Basic Research and Implications for Educational Practice*, Henry L. Roediger, III, and Jeffrey D. Karpicke, Washington University in St. Louis)

10. Truman Capote, *In Cold Blood* (New York: Random House, 1965), 5.

11. George Orwell, *Nineteen Eighty-Four* (New York: Buccaneer Books, 1949), 303.

12. Ibid., 304.

13. Ibid., 311.

14. Ibid., 312.

15. The three slogans of the Party in *Nineteen Eighty-Four* are: War Is Peace, Freedom Is Slavery, Ignorance Is Strength.

16. Ibid., 51.

17. Ibid., 52.

18. Ibid., 53.

19. Edmund Morris, *The Rise of Theodore Roosevelt* (New York: Ballantine Books, 1979), 730.

20. Benjamin Franklin, *The Autobiography of Benjamin Franklin* (New York: Buccaneer Books, 1984), 16.

21. Richard Lingeman, *Sinclair Lewis: Rebel from Main Street* (New York: Random House, 2002), 9.

22. William Manchester, *The Last Lion: Winston Spencer Churchill: Visions of Glory, 1874-1932* (Boston: Little, Brown and Company, 1983), 140.

23. Ibid., 161-162.

24. Ibid., 6.

25. Ibid., 31.

26. Fred Kaplan, *Lincoln: The Biography of a Writer* (New York: HarperCollins, 2008), 17.

27. Ibid., 18.

28. Ibid., 19.

29. Ibid., 19.

30. Ibid., 59.

31. Frederick Douglass, *Narrative of the Life of Frederick Douglass, An American Slave* (New York: Random House, 2000), 44.

32. Alex Haley, *The Autobiography of Malcolm X as Told to Alex Haley* (New York: Ballantine Books, 1964), 198.

33. Rick Atkinson, *An Army at Dawn: The War in North Africa, 1942-1943* (New York: Henry Holt and Company, 2002), 1.

34. Timothy B. Tyson, *Blood Done Sign My Name* (New York: Crown Publishers, 2004), 1.

35. Bill Bryson, *Shakespeare: The World as a Stage* (New York: Harper Perennial, 2007), 107.

36. Stephen King, *On Writing* (New York: Scribner, 2000), 236.

ABOUT THE AUTHOR

James Parkinson is a prominent southern California attorney. Mr. Parkinson began his legal practice in 1976 after receiving his law degree from Brigham Young University. He is a member of numerous professional associations and has been the recipient of many awards, including the Association of Trial Lawyers of America Citation for Excellence in 2003 and again in 2004; the National Jefferson Award for Public Service in 2007, and, in 2008, the Federal Bar Association Defender of the Constitution Award for the Inland Empire. In 2006, the J. Reuben Clark Law School of Brigham Young University named Mr. Parkinson as its Honored Alumni of the Year. He is the author, with Wilbur Colom, of the book *Turning Red States Blue: Obama's Mission to Win the Republican Vote,* which was published by Genesis Press in 2008 and, with Lee Benson, of *Soldier Slaves: Abandoned by the White House, Courts and Congress,* for which its authors were awarded the 2006 Naval Institute Press Author of the Year Award. Mr. Parkinson also co-authored *The Third Source, A Message of Hope for Education* with Dustin Hull Heuston in 2011; and in 2012 he co-authored, with Billy Casper and Lee Benson *The Big Three and Me.* In addition, Mr. Parkinson is the producer and narrator of the Ashley Karras film *The Inheritance of War,* which was based on his book, *Soldier Slaves.* Mr. Parkinson and his wife, Susan, the parents of four children, live in southern California.